You Can Be a Soul Winner — Here's How!

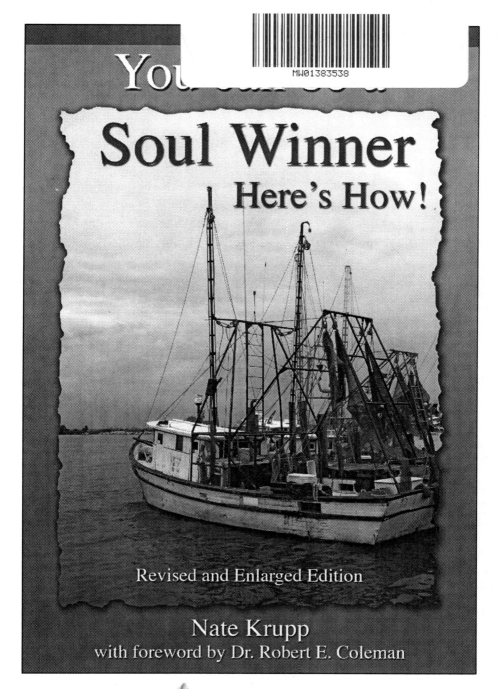

Revised and Enlarged Edition

Nate Krupp
with foreword by Dr. Robert E. Coleman

PREPARING THE WAY
Publishers

"Making ready a
people for the Lord."
Luke 1:17

2121 Barnes Avenue SE • Salem, OR 97306 USA

Scripture quotations are taken from the New American Standard translation (hereafter NASB) unless otherwise indicated.

Preparing the Way Publishers edition 2004

Copyright ©1962
by Nate Krupp

Over 60,000 copies in print

Published by

**2121 Barnes Avenue SE
Salem, OR 97306 USA**

All rights reserved. No part of this book may be reproduced, translated, stored in a retrieval system or transmitted in any form by any means, whether electronic, mechanical, photocopying, recording or otherwise, without prior written permission from the copyright holder.

Scripture taken from the New American Standard Bible, copyright 1960, 1962, 1963, 1971, 1972, 1973, 1975, 1977, 1987, 1988, The Lockman Foundation. Used by permission.

Permission to translate this book in its entirety into other languages will be granted by the author upon request to: Nate Krupp, 2121 Barnes Avenue SE, Salem, OR 97306, USA; telephone 503-585-4054, fax 503-375-8401, email kruppnj@open.org

Cover photography and design: Clint Crittenden

ISBN 1-929451-13-X
Library of Congress Control Number 0892210508

Printed in the United States of America

Dedication

Dedicated to the people of God whose hearts are burdened to see the Church return to her New Testament mission, power, and pattern in order to *get the gospel to every person in the world in this generation.*

Acknowledgements

This book is the result of thirty years (1957-1987) of soul winning and soul-winning training work with individuals and churches of many denominations. It also included five years (1965-1970) of door-to-door evangelism in a number of diverse neighborhoods in Chicago. And it included teaching personal evangelism in Youth With A Mission schools around the world (1976-1987). There was a whole team of us, known as Lay Evangelism, Inc., who were involved in this work together. I am very grateful for the many that we had the privilege of working with in this ministry.

We are very grateful to those who labored on this present edition: Carol Preston who typed the manuscript and Clint and Judy Crittenden who perfected it for publication. What a joy to work with you three!

Memorial

We are deeply indebted to Darlene Wilcox who gathered funds from her friends and relatives to publish this new edition as a memorial to her late husband Glenn Wilcox who went home to be with the Lord on January 22, 2003. He said the closing prayer at a church in Texas after several days of teaching, and God took him! He was one of the most zealous men for God and souls that this author has ever known and was a vital part of Lay Evangelism from its earliest years. He was a great inspiration to me personally and to thousands of others. May God raise up millions around the world to take his place.

Introducing the Author

Nate Krupp has been leading people to Jesus Christ and mobilizing others for soul winning since 1957. He grew up in Fostoria, Ohio, and was converted to Jesus Christ in March, 1957, in a hamburger shop through the witnessing efforts of a college student and business man during his senior year at Purdue University. He graduated the same year with a Bachelor of Science degree in Mechanical Engineering from Purdue, where he was student body president and named "Outstanding Midshipman" of his Navy R.O.T.C. Battalion.

He was discipled by the Navigators while he was an officer in the United States Navy's Civil Engineer Corps, 1957-59. This was followed by further training with the Navigators, 1959-1960; at Marion College, 1960-1961; and with Campus Crusade for Christ the summer of 1961. He married Joanne Sheets Brannon in 1961. They have been together in full-time Christian ministry since then.

Nate began local church Lay Evangelism Training work in the fall of 1961 under the auspices of the Church Extension and Evangelism Department of the Wesleyan Methodist Church. He founded Lay Evangelism, Incorporated, in 1963 to meet the growing number of requests for materials and ministry from other denominations and conducted Lay Evangelism Training Crusades with churches of many denominations throughout North America.

From 1976 to 1981 and from 1983 to 1987 he and Joanne were associated with Youth With A Mission, teaching evangelism and other subjects at their training schools on every continent. They pastored a Foursquare Church in Salem, Oregon, from 1981 to 1983.

Nate was the Evangelism Seminar Director for the Christian Holiness Association and Vice-Chairman of the Laymen's Council of the National Association of Evangelicals. He is the author of over twenty books and booklets. Nate and Joanne currently live in Salem, Oregon, where they oversee the work of Preparing the Way Publishers.

vi

Foreword

Soul winning is at the very heart of the Christian life. It is the gospel in action—the demonstration of the love of God shed abroad in the heart through the Holy Spirit.

As such, evangelism becomes a labor of love issuing from the broken heart of everyone who knows that Christ died for their sins. If there is no witness to this fact then one might wonder if it is true. A gospel that does not gladden the hearts of its adherents and make them eager to share their joy of salvation with another is manifestly no gospel at all. It must be told if indeed it is *good news*.

Yet all too often Christian people hesitate to speak out for Christ, let alone become a soul winner for their Master. Sometimes they try to dodge their Christian privileges and obligations by thinking that soul winning belongs only to a few pious saints or clergymen in the church. But more likely they see through the presumption of this position, and are honestly disturbed because they do not more conscientiously witness for their Lord. For them, the problem is not so much in wanting to do it, but in knowing what to do.

I am glad to say that this book speaks to their need. It is full of practical help in how to develop them in turn to be soul winners.

The author is not primarily concerned with theory. He wants action. He is for what works, and in that concern, he outlines simple methods and techniques based on Scriptural principles which can be learned easily by any Christian. That they will work has been demonstrated by thousands of people who have gone out to witness using these methods in Lay Evangelism Crusades across the United States and Canada.

Mr. Nate Krupp, however, wisely recognizes that soul winning is not basically a matter of methodology. It is the work of the Holy Spirit, and any success in bringing men to Christ can be attributed to the degree that the Spirit of God has control of the situation. That is why it is so important for the soul winner to be delivered from his self-cen-

vii

teredness and filled with the Holy Spirit. This is the secret of effective service which all great soul winners must learn. By stressing this condition, the author has given us the key to New Testament evangelism.

I appreciate the spiritual realism undergirding the down-to-earth approach of this book. It is methodical. It is concise. Anyone can understand it. What is more, the book breathes with the earnest sincerity of one dedicated to the cause which he represents—the cause of evangelism—the cause for which Christ has commissioned His Church to go and proclaim the gospel to the ends of the earth and until the end of time. This book can help us fulfill our calling better, and for that reason it is a pleasure to commend it to your reading, thorough study, and continued application.

Dr. Robert E. Coleman
Soul winner, Author, and Seminary Professor

Preface

The world's population continues to explode, moving toward the 10 billion mark. It is estimated that between two and three billion of these have never heard the gospel of our Lord Jesus Christ even one time. Only about ten percent of the people of the world are truly born again. Over fifty million souls will die this year. The majority of these have never heard the message of Christ. Think of it—millions of souls going into eternity every year without Christ. They live in Africa, in Asia, and right across the street.

Almost 2,000 years ago God, through the atoning death of His Son, provided a way of salvation from sin for every person. The Lord Jesus during His earthly ministry founded the Church to continue His work on earth after His ascension. To this Church He gave a task: to communicate the Good News to every person in the world in every generation (Mk. 16:15). To these first disciples also was given the Holy Spirit to equip them for this task.

The Lord Jesus additionally gave a pattern of evangelism. By His life and teachings He plainly outlined that the work of evangelism was to be done by everybody (not just pastors and evangelists), done everywhere (not just at the church building or disciples' meeting place), and done all the time (not just a few weeks out of the year). And this evangelism work was to be done as the disciples were Spirit-filled and trained.

These early disciples greatly touched the entire civilized world (Acts 17:6) and totally evangelized some portions (Acts 19:10; 1 Th. 1:8). This was done because (1) they meant business about the task, (2) they were filled with the Holy Spirit, (3) they followed the pattern, and (4) the evangelized were soon evangelizing. All of this without our modern means of communication and transportation, without the printing press, without even the written New Testament, without church buildings, without denominations, without programs, and without a thousand things we think we absolutely must have.

ix

Today, our world is about to explode. Sin abounds on every hand. Millions stand on the brink of hell. Our Lord's return draws near. Never in the world's history has there been a time when there was a greater need for getting the gospel of the Lord Jesus Christ out to the unsaved multitudes. The night comes when no man can work. The need of the hour is for the Church of Jesus Christ (1) to see anew her God-given purpose, (2) to experience afresh her God-given power, and (3) to begin to follow her God-given pattern. This is no time for playing church. We must put the mission of getting the gospel of Jesus Christ to every person in the world in this generation as our primary task. We must go to our knees in our closets of prayer and our upper rooms to seek, find, and maintain the Spirit-dominated life. The time has come when the office desk, the factory work-bench, the home, and a thousand other places must become pulpits and every Christian an effective, Spirit-filled evangelist.

Since 1961 I have been training pastors and laymen to be personal soul winners in order to effect a return to true New Testament evangelism. From the beginning the Lord blessed this ministry with wonderful results. Churches were transformed. Pastors began leading their people into the harvest fields. Thousand of laymen have become effective, Spirit-filled personal soul winners, and many people have found Jesus Christ as their Savior and Lord. For all of this we praise the Lord. But it is just the beginning of what we believe He wants to do.

The first edition of this book was written in 1962 because we were not able to find any book in print which gave all of the necessary, scriptural, practical, simple "how" for all areas necessary to mobilize and train Christians to become effective, Spirit-filled, personal soul winners. That edition was a result of five years of personal soul-winning experience, months at the job of training scores of Christians to do personal soul winning, consultation and working with great contemporary soul winners, and the study of soul-winning books then available.

A revised and enlarged edition was done in 1988 and was the result of an additional twenty-five years of experience of mobilizing Christians for various types of personal and small-group evangelism. This present PTWP edition, done in 2004, is a final up-date.

This book can be used by the individual believer who desires to become an effective soul winner, as a text in a church-wide personal evangelism training program, and as a study guide for men's, women's, and youth groups. It can be used in conventions, seminars, and retreats on soul winning and as the study text for a practical course in personal evangelism at Bible schools, Christian colleges and seminaries.

This book is not written for those who are simply desirous to learn more about Christian service. Rather, it is written for the sincere, born-again person who is openheartedly desirous to know how to get started in the greatest task in the world. It is written for the Christian who will count the cost of being a true disciple (Lk. 14:33) as it relates to fulfilling the Great Commission. And then, having counted the cost, will walk in the light (1 Jn. 1:7).

The harvest is truly plenteous, the laborers few, and the time short. It is my earnest prayer that the Lord of the harvest will use this book to bring about a return to true New Testament evangelism, and to thrust millions of believers on every continent into the white harvest fields while there is yet time. May God be glorified as you study this book and begin to live the wonderful life of a soul winner.

—Nate Krupp

xii

Contents

Introduction 15

PART ONE — Prepare to Win Souls 17

    Chapter 1 – Get a Vision 19

    Chapter 2 – Experience the Spirit-filled Life 25

    Chapter 3 – Learn a Soul Winning Plan 45

    Chapter 4 – Learn a Home Visitation Procedure........75

    Chapter 5 – Obtain Soul Winning Equipment 87

PART TWO — Begin to Win Souls 91

    Chapter 6 – Locate Evangelism Prospects 93

    Chapter 7 – Pray for Your Prospects 109

    Chapter 8 – Cultivate Your Prospects 115

    Chapter 9 – Present Christ to Your Prospects...........117

    Chapter 10 – Conserve the Fruit of Evangelism 133

PART THREE — Continue to Win Souls 143

    Chapter 11 – Train Others 145

    Chapter 12 – Keep Going 149

APPENDICES

    A – Definitions 153

    B – Standards for Soul Winners 154

    C – Sample Prospect Card......................................155

    D – Witnessing Assignment Sheet 157

    E – Community Religious Survey–Door-to-Door 158

    F – Community Religious Survey–Telephone 159

    G – Reaching Cities for Christ 160

    H – Recommended Reading 161

    I – Outstanding Quotations about Soul Winning 164

    J – Other Helpful Materials from PTWP 175

xiii

xiv

Introduction

You are a born-again Christian. The Lord wants to make you a fisher of men—"Follow me, and I will make you fishers of men" (Mt. 4:19).

This is the purpose for which you have been saved—". . . I chose you, and appointed you, that you should go and bear fruit, and that your fruit should remain . . ." (Jn. 15:16).

This is a test of your discipleship—"By this is My Father glorified, that you bear much fruit, and so prove to be My disciples" (Jn. 15:8).

And He wants to give you the necessary power—"But you shall receive power when the Holy Spirit has come upon you; and you shall be My witnesses . . ." (Acts 1:8).

This is one of the most wonderful days in your life—you are starting down the road to becoming an effective, Spirit-filled, personal soul winner!

First you must prepare for this great work.

You must—

- Get a vision

- Experience the Spirit-filled life

- Learn a soul winning plan

- Learn a home visitation procedure

- Obtain soul-winning equipment

You can be a Soul Winner — Here's How!

Then you must get started in this wonderful task.

You must—

- Locate evangelism prospects

- Pray for your prospects

- Cultivate your prospects

- Present Christ to your prospects

- Conserve the fruit of evangelism.

And finally you must continue—live the rest of your life as an effective, Spirit-filled, personal soul winner. Then mobilize others to become the same.

You can be a Soul Winner—Here's How!

Chapter 1

Get a Vision

The Bible says, *"Where there is no vision, the people perish . . ."* (Prov. 29:18). A million people die every week around the world. Most of them do not know the Lord. Right here in this country there are people passing into eternity every day. Many of them do not know Jesus. Could it be that these multitudes are perishing without Christ today because you do not have your spiritual vision clearly in focus? Do you really see as God sees? Are the eternal truths of God revealed in His Word the dominating guideposts of your life?

What you believe determines what you do. And, what you believe determines what you become. You must get your spiritual eyes focused on things eternal. Your every thought, word, decision, and action must be made with eternity in plain sight.

Your first step, therefore, in becoming an effective, Spirit-filled, personal soul winner is to get a vision.

I. A VISION OF THE REAL CONDITION OF MEN WITHOUT CHRIST

How much do you believe in the reality and the consequences of sin? Do you really believe that men and women without Jesus Christ are lost? That they are without God in this life? That they will spend forever in hell in the next life?

The Bible says that all men live a life of sin (Rom. 3:9-10, 23). They have sinned by transgressing the law of God (1 Jn. 3:4), by unbelief (Rom. 14:23), and by not doing that which they know to be right (Jas. 4:17).

Because of sin, men are spiritually dead right in this life (Eph. 2:1; 1 Tim. 5:6). They are already under the control of Satan (Acts 26:18; 2 Cor. 4:4). And they are under the wrath of God (Rom. 1:18; Jn. 3:36). Truly, they are as sheep without a shepherd (Mt. 9:36; 1 Pet. 2:25).

You can be a Soul Winner — Here's How!

Our job is not to try to reform people. But to love them, share the Good News with them, and see them transformed by the power of God.

Because of sin, men will spend forever with the devil and his angels (Mt. 25:41) in everlasting punishment and destruction (2 Th. 1:9) in the lake of fire (Rev. 20:15). I wonder sometimes, how much we really believe in hell. If we did, I'm convinced that our lives, and the lives of our churches would be different.

Get alone with God and meditate on the truths set forth in these passages of Scripture. Let these truths get ahold of your heart. Ask God to break your heart and fill it with compassion for a world that is lost.

II. A VISION OF OUR RESPONSIBILITY

The second thing we need to catch a vision of is our responsibility. God only has one way to reach the lost—*His people*. To us He has committed or entrusted the gospel (1 Cor. 9:17; 1 Th. 2:4). To us He has given a command to proclaim this Good News to *every living person in the entire world in every generation* (Mk. 16:15).

When we look at the Great Commission as outlined in Mt. 28:18-20, Mk. 16:15-20, Lk. 24:45-49, Jn. 20:21-23, and Acts 1:4-8, we find that it is actually a six-fold task:

A. Seek to be endued with power by the infilling of the Holy Spirit (Lk. 24:49 and Acts 1:8).

B. Go to the lost.

The imperative of *going* to the lost is brought out in each of these five Great Commission passages. It is *not* the lost coming to the church to hear the gospel. It is the *Church going* to the lost with the Good News. Luke 14:21-23 gives us an interesting pattern. Here Jesus said first "go into the streets and lanes of the city." Then He said "go into the highways." If we would evangelize our cities—then cover all of the houses between our cities—we would evangelize the entire nation—and world. We must GO to *every* home on *every* street and road in *every* city and county in *every* nation on earth in *every* generation.

20

GET A VISION

C. We are to go to the lost for the purpose of *communicating the gospel* to them.

Our Lord did not say that we were to go and tell them about our church or pastor or programs or theological distinctions. Nor are we to try to reform them. But He has said that we are to go for the purpose of telling them the Good News. Going where they are, accepting and loving them like they are, and telling them about Jesus and His authority to forgive their sins and His power to transform their lives. We are to communicate or explain the Good News in such a way that the lost understands it and knows what he has to do about it.

D. We are to *lead to the Lord* those who are ready to respond.

We are to take this Good News to every person. Some will respond and some won't. Those who are ready to respond we are to lead to the Lord in an experience of repentance toward God and faith in our Lord Jesus Christ (Acts 20:21).

E. Those who respond to the gospel in true repentance and faith we are to *baptize* (Mt. 28:19, Mk. 16:16, Acts 2:38, etc.).

F. To these new converts we then are to *teach everything* that Jesus has taught us—"teaching them to obey everything I have commanded you" (Mt. 28:20, NIV).

That's the job God has given us to do. It's the only job He's given us to do. And until we do it, the blood of the lost is on our hands (Ezek. 3:18). This is *the task* of the Church. We need to get a vision of this.

Another thing that we need to catch a vision of is that the Great Commission is *a personal commission*. Sin is personal. Salvation is personal. The infilling of the Holy Spirit is personal. Our daily walk with Jesus is personal. And so is the Great Commission. It is a *personal command* from Jesus Christ to each one of His followers to go *into their personal world* and communicate the Good News. You are to be a witness, both in your community and to the ends of the earth (Acts 1:8). You are chosen and ordained by the Lord Jesus Christ (1) to go, (2) to bring forth fruit, and (3) to

You can be a Soul Winner—Here's How!

conserve your fruit (Jn. 15:16). God's primary way to reach the lost in your community, in your county, is through His people who live there. France will basically be evangelized by the Christians in France. Chicago will be evangelized by God's people in Chicago—as they are challenged, trained and sent out. **You** must evangelize your community and nation and world.

There is only one reason why the Great Commission has never been fulfilled: God's people—you and I—have not fulfilled it. But *we can* in this generation! Let's seek God for a heart-breaking, life-changing vision of our responsibility.

III. A VISION OF HOW TO FULFILL OUR RESPONSIBILITY

Winning the lost to Christ is not a matter of gimmicks, techniques, or man-made programs. It involves following God-ordained and therefore God-blessed principles. He has very plainly set forth exactly what we must do and how we are to go about our task of getting the gospel effectively communicated to unsaved people and of bringing them into a vital, personal relationship with the Savior. Let's see exactly what is involved in fulfilling our responsibility. Then let's get at the job.

You must first die to self (Mt. 16:24) and all that is a part of this life (Lk. 14:33; 2 Tim. 2:4). You must yield everything that is a part of your life to God (Phil. 3:8; Rom. 12:1) for His use in getting the message of Christ to every person on the face of the globe.

You must urgently (Jn. 9:4) seek the lost (Lk. 19:10). You must fast and pray for the lost (Mt. 17:21; Isa. 66:8). You must weep over the lost (Ps. 126:5-6). You must be a servant to them (1 Cor. 9:19-22). You must take the message of salvation to them (Mk. 16:15). And you must urge them to come to Christ (2 Cor. 5:20).

As you go at this many-fold task, you need to pray for boldness (Acts 4:29), for open doors (Col. 4:3), and for wisdom (Jas. 1:5). And you must be as wise as a serpent, harmless as a dove (Mt. 10:16), and bold as a lion (Prov. 28:1).

GET A VISION

To put it another way, we are to:

A. Prepare the soil.

We prepare the soil by allowing God's love to flow through us out to others and by praying for people.

B. Sow seed daily.

If we sow bountifully we'll reap bountifully. Sow all the seed you can in every way possible every day.

C. Water seed that is already sown.

D. Pick the fruit that is ripe.

But don't pick it before it is ripe!

E. Conserve the fruit.

Take care of the fruit.

F. Care for the vineyard.

Use wisdom as you're in the vineyard so that you will have a harvest in the future also.

IV. A VISION OF GOD'S PART

Your task of evangelism will seem almost impossible unless you catch a glimpse of God's part. He is a great God. He has made provision for the preparation of the harvest. And He has made provision for the preparation of the harvester or laborer.

God has given you a weapon—the Word of God—for your work (Mk. 4:14; Eph. 6:17). Use it. It is a devouring fire (Jer. 5:14), a strong hammer (Jer. 23:29), and a two-edged sword (Heb. 4:12).

The Holy Spirit will empower you for the task (Lk. 24:49), teach you what to do (Jn. 14:26), and direct you as you go (Acts 8:29).

He has given you the promise of His presence as you go to take the message of salvation to your unsaved friends (Mt. 28:20). As the Amplified New Testament puts it, ". . . lo, I am with you all the days,—perpetually, uniformly, and on every occasion . . ."

How many of us believe that there's power in the Word of God? How many of us believe that when we go up to knock on a door, that Jesus will be right there at our side? And that when we open our mouths to speak, the Holy Spirit will anoint us and give us

23

You can be a Soul Winner — Here's How!

boldness and the words to say, and make what we have to say effective and fruitful? We say we believe these things, and theoretically I'm sure we do, but do we really? What more do we need?

As you go, filled with the Spirit and armed with the Word, to the lost with the message of Christ, God will open their hearts to the truth (Acts 16: 14). He will convict them of their sin (Jn. 16:8; Acts 24:25). He will reveal Jesus Christ to them (Jn. 8:18, 15:26), and as they respond He will save them (Rom. 10:13; 2 Pet. 3:9).

What more do you need?

Questions to Answer
 1. What are the consequences of sin?
 2. What is your evangelism responsibility?
 3. What must you do in order to bring someone to Jesus Christ?

Questions for Meditation and Application
 1. How much do you care for a world that is lost and without Christ? How much are you really committed to the task of getting the gospel to every person in this generation? What changes do you purpose to make?
 2. Considering all that you must do to lead someone to Christ (question 3 above), what progress are you making with your unsaved friends? What are your plans for the coming month? Year?
 3. Considering all that God has done to make your witnessing and soul winning efforts successful, how much of His provision are you experiencing? What do you purpose to see Him do through you in the coming year?

Assignments
 1. Look up and meditate on each Scripture reference given in this chapter.
 2. Begin to pray that God will fill your heart with a compassion for those around you without Christ.

Chapter 2

Experience the Spirit-filled Life

Your second step in becoming an effective soul winner is to experience the Spirit-filled life. The lukewarm, carnal, unfruitful Christian can become a vital, dynamic soul winner by experiencing the Spirit-filled life.

I. REALIZE THAT THERE IS AN EXPERIENCE OF BEING FILLED WITH THE HOLY SPIRIT.

A. Who the Holy Spirit is.

The Holy Spirit is the third person of the Trinity: Father, Son, and Holy Spirit. He is a person equal in every way with the Father and the Son. He has infinite intellect (1 Cor. 2:11), emotion (Rom. 15:30), and will (1 Cor. 12:11).

More about what He is like is found by studying His names: Spirit of God (1 Cor. 3:16), Spirit of Life (Rom. 8:2), Spirit of Faith (2 Cor. 4:13), Spirit of Truth (Jn. 16:13), Spirit of Grace (Heb. 10:29), and Spirit of Holiness (Rom. 1:4).

The Holy Spirit has come for the two-fold purpose of glorifying the Lord Jesus (Jn. 16:13-14) and directing the Church in its mission of world evangelization (Mt. 9:38).

B. The impartation of spiritual life.

The Bible teaches *two basic works* of the Spirit. *First* there is the *impartation of life* that takes place at the time of conversion to Jesus Christ when the Holy Spirit imparts life to the human spirit. John calls it being *born again*, or *born of the Spirit* (Jn. 3:3-8). This great ministry of the Holy Spirit's imparting life is also mentioned in Ezek. 32:26, Jn. 1:13, 6:63, 2 Cor. 3:6, 5:17, Eph. 2:1, Ti. 3:5, 1 Pet. 1:23, 1 Jn. 5:1, etc. It is this experience that places one within the Kingdom of God.

You can be a Soul Winner — Here's How!

C. What the Holy Spirit does for every Christian.

At the time that the Holy Spirit imparts life to a person, He also performs the following ministries:

1. *He comes to dwell with you.*

   "However you are not in the flesh but in the Spirit, if indeed the Spirit of God dwells in you. But if anyone does not have the Spirit of Christ, he does not belong to Him" (Rom. 8:9)

2. *He gives you the assurance that you are a child of God.*

   "The Spirit Himself bears witness with our spirit that we are the children of God" (Rom. 8:16).

3. *He places you into the Body of Christ.*

   "For even as the body is one and yet has many members, and all the members of the body, though they are many, are one body, so also is Christ. For by one Spirit we were all baptized into one body, whether Jews or Greeks, whether slaves or free, and we were all made to drink of one Spirit" (1 Cor. 12:12-13).

4. *He gives you the power to stop practicing a life of sin.*

   "No one who is born of God practices sin, because His seed abides in him; and he cannot sin, because he is born of God" (1 Jn. 3:9).

5. *He begins to teach you the Bible.*

   "But the Helper, the Holy Spirit, whom the Father will send in My name, He will teach you all things, and bring to your remembrance all that I said to you" (Jn. 14:26).

What a wonderful experience—being born of the Spirit!

D. The additional experience of being baptized or filled with the Holy Spirit.

In addition to the impartation of spiritual life, there is a *second* basic ministry of the Holy Spirit, that being His filling ministry to the believer which is an *enduement with power* for service. We find this mentioned a number of places in the Scriptures, ie., Mt. 3:11, Lk. 24:49, Acts 1:8, 2:4, 2:33, 4:8, 4:31, 6:8, 8:14-17, 9:17, 10:44-47, 19:2-6, Gal. 3:14, etc.

EXPERIENCE THE SPIRIT-FILLED LIFE

1. *The disciples after Pentecost were filled with the Spirit.*

   "And they were all filled with the Holy Spirit . . ." (Acts 2:4). "Then Peter, filled with the Holy Spirit, said . . ." (Acts 4:8). See also Acts 4:31, 7:55, 11:24, 13:9, 13:52.

2. *Paul's writings teach that the Christian is to be filled with the Spirit.*

   In the letter to the Christians at Ephesus, he mentions that he is praying that they "may be filled up to all the fullness of God" (3:19). Later in the letter, he commands them to have this experience—"be filled with the Spirit" (5:18).

3. *The world's outstanding Christians testify to an experience of being filled with the Holy Spirit.*

   a. George Muller—"I became a believer in the Lord Jesus in the beginning of November, 1825. For the first four years afterward, it was for a good part in great weakness; but in July, 1829, it came with me to an entire and full surrender of heart. I gave myself fully to the Lord."

   b. Charles G. Finney—"But as I turned and was about to take a seat by the fire, I received a mighty baptism of the Holy Ghost . . . No words can express the wonderful love that was shed abroad in my heart."

   c. John Wesley—"About three in the morning, as we were continuing instant in prayer, the power of God came mightily upon us, insomuch that many cried out for exceeding joy, and many fell to the ground."

   d. Dwight L. Moody—"I was crying all the time that God would fill me with His Spirit. Well, one day, in the city of New York—oh, what a day! I cannot describe it, I seldom refer to it; it is almost too sacred an experience to name . . . I only say that God revealed Himself to me, and I had such an experience of his love that I had to ask Him to stay His hand."

You can be a Soul Winner — Here's How!

4. *Various terminology used.*

Various terminology is used with reference to this *enduement with power.* In Mt. 3:11, Acts 1:5, and 11:16 it's called the *baptism of the Holy Spirit.* In Acts 4:8, 4:31, and 9:17 it's called being *filled with the Spirit.* In Lk. 24:49 it's *being endued (or clothed) with power from on high.* Acts 1:8, 8:16, 10:44, and 11:15 use the term the Holy Spirit *falling* or *coming upon* the believer. In Acts 2:38, 10:45, and 15:8 it's the *gift of the Holy Spirit.* In Lk. 24:49, Acts 1:4, and 2:33 it's the *promise of the Father.* Acts 2:17, 2:33, and 10:45 use the term *pour.*

5. *What it means to be filled with the Spirit.*

Although the terminology used varies according to the different theological backgrounds, the results in experience and life are basically the same. To be filled with the Holy Spirit is to be controlled by Him rather than by self. The Spirit-filled Christian is cleansed, possessed, led, and empowered by the Holy Spirit. He has possession and mastery of the human spirit.

II. RECOGNIZE YOUR NEED TO BE FILLED WITH THE HOLY SPIRIT

There are five reasons or purposes for or results of being filled with the Holy Spirit.

A. To cleanse the inner man.

In Acts 15:8-9 the Scriptures talk about the cleansing of the heart by the Spirit: "And God, who knows the heart, bore witness to them, giving them the Holy Spirit, just as He also did to us; and He made no distinction between us and them, cleansing their hearts by faith."

B. To give power to enable the Christian to live a victorious Christian life.

Romans 8, Galatians 5:16, 5:25, etc., talk about the life of victory that is available to the believer who is filled with the Spirit. There is a wonderful, victorious Christian life that many Christians personally know, but that many more do not

EXPERIENCE THE SPIRIT-FILLED LIFE

know. This is a life which you must have if you are ever to become an effective soul winner. Your life speaks louder than your words. You must have a life which will cause others to want your Savior. You are His ambassador (2 Cor. 3:2, 5:20).

1. *Your present, defeated Christian life.*

   Paul talked about a time of defeat in his own Christian experience when he could not do the things he knew to be right (Rom. 7:19). Maybe that's your story. Do any of these apply to your life?

   a. A love of human praise

   b. An exalted feeling of your own importance

   c. Anger

   d. Jealousness

   e. Being critical of others

   f. Lustful desires

   g. Fearfulness

   h. Selfishness

   i. Frustration

   j. Sensitiveness

   k. Impatience

   l. Stubbornness

   m. Indifference

   n. Unbelief

2. *The victorious life God wants to give you.*

   "You shall love the Lord your God with all your heart, with all your soul, and with all your mind. This is the great and foremost commandment. And a second is like it, You shall love your neighbor as yourself" (Mt. 22: 37-39).

   "Rejoice in the Lord always; . . . Be anxious for nothing, but in everything by prayer and supplication with thanksgiving let your requests be made known to God. And the peace of God, which surpasses all comprehen-

You can be a Soul Winner — Here's How!

sion, shall guard your hearts and your minds in Christ Jesus" (Phil. 4:4, 6-7).

"Rejoice always; pray without ceasing; in everything give thanks; for this is God's will for you in Christ Jesus" (1 Th. 5:16-18).

This life of victory becomes yours as you are filled with God's Spirit.

C. To give witnessing and soul-winning power.

A third purpose for being filled with the Spirit is to provide spiritual power for evangelism. In Lk. 24:49, when Jesus gave the Great Commission, He said, "And behold, I am sending forth the promise of my Father upon you; but you are to stay in the city until you are clothed with power from on high." In Acts 1:8 we read, "You shall receive power when the Holy Spirit has come upon you; and you shall be My witnesses both in Jerusalem, and in all Judea and Samaria, and even to the remotest part of the earth." It is this endowment with power that turns the defeated, fruitless Christian life into one of victory, power, and fruitfulness.

1. *The defeated Christian.*

   Are you like the disciples before Pentecost, who, at the crucial hour of the Lord's betrayal at Gethsemane, "forsook Him, and fled" (Mt. 26:56)? Or, like Peter who "followed him afar off" (26:58) and then, at the witnessing and soul-winning opportunity, said "I do not know the man" (26:72)? God has better things in store for you.

2. *The empowered Christian life God wants you to have.*

   "And when they had prayed, the place where they had gathered together was shaken, and they were all filled with the Holy Spirit, and began to speak the word of God with boldness" (Acts 4:31).

   This transformation comes when one is filled with the Spirit.

EXPERIENCE THE SPIRIT-FILLED LIFE

D. To provide the fruit of the Spirit.

The fourth purpose for being filled with the Spirit is that there might flow from our lives the fruit of the Spirit as listed in Gal. 5:22-23: "love, joy, peace, patience, kindness, goodness, faithfulness, gentleness, self-control." We all would like to have those qualities flowing out from our lives wouldn't we? God's way for us to have them is for the Holy Spirit to be in control of our life. We can try all day to have love. We can try all day to have joy. We can try all day to have patience. But we won't have them by human trying. We get these qualities by being filled with the Spirit. When He is in control, the fruit automatically appears. And to the degree that He is in control of our life, to that degree these qualities, these characteristics, this fruit will flow from our lives.

E. To provide the gifts of the Spirit.

The fifth purpose for being filled with the Spirit is to open the door to the operation of various gifts of the Spirit. Rom. 12 and 1 Cor. 12 list seventeen various ways that the Holy Spirit wants to gift, or equip, His people. These gifts include prophecy, service, teaching, exhorting, giving, leading, showing mercy, the word of wisdom, the word of knowledge, faith, gifts of healings, the effecting of miracles, the distinguishing of spirits, various kinds of tongues, the interpretation of tongues, helps, and administrations. These are ways that the Holy Spirit may want to sovereignly gift any one of us to be a more effective servant of Christ—that we might more effectively minister to one another and to the world.

Seek God for the infilling of the Holy Spirit. Then allow Him to gift and use you as He would choose!

III. MEET GOD'S REQUIREMENTS FOR BEING FILLED WITH THE HOLY SPIRIT

You are now entering the most exciting and important section of this chapter—the section which outlines the seven steps you can take to experience the infilling of the Holy Spirit.

You can be a Soul Winner — Here's How!

A. Steps of preparation.

Receiving God's Spirit in His fullness is nothing to rush into lightly. There first must come the preparation of the vessel before it is to be filled. So we start with five steps of preparation.

1. *Recognize your need of being filled with the Holy Spirit.*

   God always meets us at the point of our need. He will fill you with His Spirit when you recognize your need of this gracious experience.

   So away with pride and all confidence in the flesh. Is your heart clean? Do you have a victorious life? Do you have the power for witnessing and soul winning? Are the gifts of the Spirit operative in your life? If you cannot say *yes* to these questions, you need to experience the infilling of God's Spirit. Recognizing this with all of your heart is the place to begin.

2. *Realize all that is involved.*

   Being Spirit-filled is allowing the Holy Spirit to have all of you. You must yield your entire being to Him—and do it without a single reservation. You must become simply His instrument. To obey Him must be your only desire in life (Acts 5:32). Being Spirit-filled involves coming to this place of absolute surrender to Him before He can take charge.

   Also, be assured that, if He has complete charge of you, He will want you to glorify Jesus, for this is one of His purposes (Jn. 16:13-14). Being Spirit-filled, therefore, also involves coming to the place in your life where you desire every area of your life to be such that it glorifies the Lord Jesus Christ.

   Being Spirit-filled also involves being the Holy Spirit's instrument for evangelism. He came to be the Lord of the Harvest (Mt. 9:38). The responsibility for a world-wide spiritual harvest is His. A surrender to Him involves a willingness to become personally, wholeheartedly involved in the task of world evangelization. You must

EXPERIENCE THE SPIRIT-FILLED LIFE

give yourself to Him for personal witnessing and soul winning, praying for the lost and for laborers, and giving abundantly of your financial means to get the gospel to every creature in this generation.

3. *Begin to seek God for the infilling of the Spirit.*

Not only do we need to see our need and realize what is involved, but we also need to definitely seek God for this experience. Jesus said, "Blessed are those who hunger and thirst for righteousness, for they shall be satisfied" (Mt. 5:6). Again, He said, "If any man is thirsty, let him come to Me and drink . . . This He spoke of the Spirit . . ." (Jn. 7:37-39). Are you hungry and thirsty for God's Spirit? Really?? Begin to seek God with all of your heart for the infilling of the Holy Spirit.

4. *Make everything right with God and with man.*

Acts 24:16 records, "In view of this, I also do my best to maintain always a blameless conscience both before God and before men." Preparation for the Spirit's control includes having a clear, blameless conscience toward God and toward people. This involves recognition, confession, restitution, and renunciation.

Get alone with God for an extended period of time. Ask Him to reveal to you (Ps. 139:23-24) all in your life that is hindering the work of the Spirit. Take along paper and pencil and make a list. Ask God to search deep into the corners of your heart and reveal everything.

With reference to your relationship with God this may include impure thoughts and motives, unholy desires, sins of omission, prayerlessness, disobedience to any known portion of the Word of God, failure to do the whole will of God with all of your heart. Then confess these things to God and ask for His forgiveness (1 Jn. 1:9).

With reference to your relationship with people this may include speaking unkindly to, gossiping about, personally offending or wronging another. Make a list. Then per-

33

You can be a Soul Winner — Here's How!

sonally go to each one and ask his forgiveness. If you cannot go, telephone or write.

The author sought without success to be filled with the Spirit for six months a few years after his conversion because he was unwilling to confess to a Christian brother that he had borrowed and broken his 50-cent knife without permission to use it or without making arrangements to pay for the damage. The real problem, of course, was pride.

True repentance involves renouncing and forsaking. It is not enough to simply confess that which displeases God. There must be a turning away from it. Even the little things that are doubtful and questionable must be forsaken. In Song 2:15 we read, "Catch the foxes for us, the little foxes that are ruining our vineyards, while our vineyards are in blossom." It's the little things (foxes) that spoil our spiritual life (vine).

All of this requires real determination and discipline. Habits of life must be changed. But the Lord will faithfully help you. At any cost, make sure that you are without offense toward God and man.

5. *Yield everything to God.*

To experience the Spirit-filled life, there must come that day in your life when you die to self. John 12:24-25 says, "Truly, truly, I say to you, unless a grain of wheat falls into the earth and dies, it remains by itself alone; but if it dies, it bears much fruit. He who loves his life loses it; and he who hates his life in this world shall keep it to life eternal." This includes all that is part of this life. Luke 14:33 states, "So, therefore, no one of you can be My disciple who does not give up all his own possessions." We must yield everything to God. Romans 12:1-2 says, "I urge you therefore, brethren, by the mercies of God, to present your bodies a living and holy sacrifice, acceptable to God, which is your spiritual service of worship. And do not be conformed to this world, but be transformed by the renewing of your mind, that you may prove what the will

EXPERIENCE THE SPIRIT-FILLED LIFE

of God is, that which is good and acceptable and perfect." Become, without reservation, the Holy Spirit's complete possession. Surrender everything to God. All must be turned over to Him—your self, your life, your time, your money, your family, your possessions, your talents, your desires, your goals, your ambitions—surrender every-thing to Him. Hold nothing back—put everything at God's disposal. Tell the Lord that everything is His to do with as He wishes.

Five steps of preparation—recognize your need of being filled with the Holy Spirit, realize all that is involved, begin to seek God for the baptism of the Spirit, make everything right with God and with man, and yield everything to Him. This prepares the vessel for the Spirit's infilling. Now on to the two steps of actual reception.

B. Steps of Reception.

1. *Ask God to fill you.*

   In Lk. 11:11-13 we read, "Now suppose one of you fathers is asked by his son for a fish; he will not give him a snake instead of a fish, will he? Or if he is asked for an egg, he will not give him a scorpion, will he? If you then, being evil, know how to give good gifts to your children, how much more shall our Heavenly Father give the Holy Spirit to those who ask Him?"

   Once you have fulfilled the steps of preparation for the Holy Spirit's coming in His fullness, simply ask God to fill you with His Spirit.

   And remember, God is on the giving end. He is more desirous that we be filled with His Spirit than we are. He wants to give us the Holy Spirit. He wants to fill us with His Spirit. He's waiting for us to prepare the vessel and then to simply ask.

2. *Receive by faith.*

   In Jn. 7, verse 37, Jesus said, "If any man is thirsty, let him *come to Me and drink.*" In verses 38 and 39 He goes on to explain that He's talking about the Holy Spirit. He invites

35

You can be a Soul Winner—Here's How!

us to come, and having come and asked, then He says, "Now, by faith, just drink!" Ask believing, ask in faith, ask without doubts or reservations—then believe that He has come. Receive Him by faith. Drink in the Holy Spirit in His fullness.

There may be an emotional experience that accompanies it or there may not be. There may be various gifts of the Spirit that accompany it. Or there may be just the quiet assurance that He has come. The things that accompany this infilling may vary. The important thing is to prepare the vessel, to ask, to receive by faith, and to know that He has come.

Right now, before going any further in this book, we urge you to get alone with God for an extended period of time. Reread this chapter and seek God earnestly for the baptism of the Holy Spirit.

Then complete the following:

On this_____day of _____in the year_____, I have met God's requirements and do believe that I have been filled with God's Spirit. The Holy Spirit now has charge of my heart and life.

_____
(signed)

In the days to come, as a result of the Holy Spirit's fullness, you will find that there will be a greater desire to witness and to win others to Christ. There will be a greater freedom and more boldness in witnessing (Acts 1:8). The fruit of the Spirit (Gal. 5:22-23) will be in greater abundance in your life. There will be greater victory in your life. And various gifts of the Spirit may become operative in your life.

What a life! Hallelujah!

EXPERIENCE THE SPIRIT-FILLED LIFE

IV. FULFILL THE CONDITIONS FOR CONTINUING THE SPIRIT-FILLED LIFE

It's one thing to be initially filled with the Spirit. But then, after this initial infilling of the Spirit, there is another matter that is just as important. That is the matter of daily walking in the Spirit. We must learn to be led daily, moment by moment, by the Holy Spirit. We must fulfill the conditions for continuing the Spirit-filled life.

A. Recognize that it is a moment-by-moment experience.

By thinking that the Spirit-filled life is a once-for-all experience, and by not receiving proper instructions after the initial infilling, many have failed to continue this wonderful life. The tragic thing is that many of these continue to believe and to profess that the Holy Spirit still has complete control of their life.

The Spirit-filled life is not a once-for-all experience. It is an experience that is maintained moment by moment. We continue the Spirit-filled life by continually meeting, moment by moment, the initial conditions or requirements. Continue to recognize, moment by moment, your need of the Spirit's control of your heart and life. Continue, moment by moment, to make sure that you are without offense toward God and toward man. Continue, moment by moment, to have an attitude of openness to His continued infilling into your life.

Remember, too, that keeping yielded to God includes a new obedience and a new yielding as the Holy Spirit reveals new truth to you (1 Jn. 1:7).

B. Begin the day with the Lord.

Being a Spirit-filled Christian does not exempt you from being in constant warfare with Satan and his forces (Eph. 6:12-13). How needful it is to begin the day in God's presence.

1. This was the practice of our Lord (Mk. 1:35).

2. This was the practice of other men of the Bible including Jacob (Gen. 28:18), Hezekiah (2 Chr. 29:20), Job (Job 1:5), and David (Ps. 57:8).

37

You can be a Soul Winner — Here's How!

3. It was also the regular practice of God's servants throughout the ages.

   a. Mr. Wesley spent two hours daily in prayer. He began at four in the morning.

   b. John Fletcher stained the walls of his room by the breath of his prayers. Sometimes he would pray all night. His whole life was a life of prayer.

   c. Luther said: "If I fail to spend two hours in prayer each morning, the devil gets the victory through the day. I have so much business I cannot get on without spending three hours daily in prayer."

   d. John Welch, the holy and wonderful Scottish preacher, thought the day ill-spent if he did not spend eight to ten hours in prayer.

4. Start with 20 to 30 minutes each morning. In a few months you will find that this will not be long enough and you will want to reserve at least an hour the first thing each morning for just you and the Lord. Those in full-time Christian service would do well to spend two hours each morning with the Lord.

   a. *Have a time of Bible reading.*

      1) First, ask the Holy Spirit's direction on your Bible reading.

         "Open my eyes, that I may behold wonderful things from Thy law" (Ps. 119:18).

      2) Read one chapter each day if you're just a beginner at morning devotions.

         Start with John's first letter (found almost at the end of the New Testament). It is very basic. And it is only five chapters in length. In five days, at a chapter a day, you can have it completely read.

      3) Next go on to the Gospel of John.

      4) Then read through The Acts of the Apostles.

      5) Then start with Matthew and go through the entire New Testament.

EXPERIENCE THE SPIRIT-FILLED LIFE

6) Then adopt a plan which will take you through the entire Bible in a year.

This requires about four chapters a day. Acquire a chart from your local Christian book store which you can follow to read through the Bible chronologically in a year.

Do not read just to learn more about the Bible. Read the Word of God in order to have a greater knowledge of and love for the Lord Jesus Christ. Read to apply the Word to your daily life (Mt. 4:4). Read slowly as you go. Underline words or phrases that stand out to you. Make notes. Meditate on what you read. Ask the Lord to speak to you through His Word. Ask yourself some questions. What does it say? What does it say to me? Look for promises to claim (2 Pet. 1:4) and commandments to obey (Jn. 14:21). Look for a verse that you can take with you to meditate on throughout the day (Ps.1:2-3; Josh. 1:8).

b. *Have a time of prayer.*

End your morning devotions with a good season of prayer.

1) Begin with a time of worshiping, praising, and thanking God for Who He is and for what He is doing (Ps. 34:1; Ps. 148). MAKE LOVE to Him (Rev. 4:11).

2) Then, complete your prayer time by interceding for others and by bringing situations in your own life to the Lord.

3) Make a list of prayer requests and watch God answer your requests. Pray big (Jer. 33:3)!

Pray for those on your prospect and follow-up lists (see Chapters 7 and 10). Pray for your pastor and your church. Begin to pray for your city, your state, your nation, and the world. Pray for a world-wide spiritual awakening. Pray that we (the Church, composed of all born-again people)

You can be a Soul Winner — Here's How!

will get the gospel to every person in the world in this generation (Mk. 16:15).

As you pray, ask in faith (Mt. 21:22), pray in Jesus' name (Jn. 14:13), pray according to His will (1 Jn. 5:14-15), and claim His promises (2 Cor. 7:1).

C. Walk through the day with the Lord.

Not only do we need to begin the day with the Lord—but then walk through the day with Him. As you walk through the day with Jesus, do these things:

1. *Keep your eyes on Jesus.*

   Heb. 12:2 says, "Looking unto Jesus . . ." Keep your eyes on the Lord as you walk through the day. Let Him be your example. Let Him be your constant friend. Don't look to other people for your Christian standards and convictions. Don't be offended at what others say and do. Don't live your life to please men. Live every moment to please God.

2. *Rest in the Lord.*

   Galatians 2:20 reads, "I have been crucified with Christ; and it is no longer I who live, but Christ lives in me; and the life which I now live in the flesh I live by faith in the Son of God, who loved me, and delivered Himself up for me." *Jesus Christ lives within you!* The Spirit-filled life is not one of struggling and trying—it is a wonderful life of trusting and resting. As you walk through the day with the Lord, simply abide in Him. Relax. Rest in the Lord. Allow Him to live His life through you. See Isa. 26:3, Jn. 15:4-5, Phil. 4:6-7, Heb. 4: 9-11, 1 Pet. 5:7.

3. *Exercise your authority.*

   We are in a battle with the hosts of heaven (Eph. 6:12). But Jesus came to render the devil and his hosts powerless (Heb. 2:14-15). You can be victorious. Exercise the authority you have as a child of God. Put on the armor of God (Eph. 6:10-18). Resist the devil (Jas. 4:7). Quote the Word to him (Lk. 4:3-13). Speak to him (Mt. 16:23). Use the name of Jesus (Lk. 10:17-20).

EXPERIENCE THE SPIRIT-FILLED LIFE

4. *Be a channel for the Holy Spirit.*

In Jn. 7:37-39 Jesus is talking about the Holy Spirit. And in verse 38 He says, "From his innermost being shall flow rivers of living water." Jesus compares the Spirit-filled Christian to a flowing river. God, the Holy Spirit, does not fill us just for our sake. But He fills us in order that He might flow through us. And He will continue to fill us as we continue to allow Him to flow through us.

So, be at His disposal, moment by moment. Listen to whatever He may whisper to you by that still, small voice. Be obedient when He says go here, or there. Do this or that. When He says speak to this person. Be a broken, available, surrendered vessel that He can flow through daily, moment by moment. Be a blessing to this person and that person. Allow the fruit of the Spirit to flow out through your life. Allow Him to flow through you in any way that He may choose to flow.

You know what happens when a river gets dammed up. The river backs up and begins to stagnate and ceases to flow. And that's the way it is in our lives if we allow things to creep in that prevent the Spirit's flowing through us. It stagnates our lives and our ministry. The Holy Spirit, moment by moment, fills us only as we allow Him to flow through us, moment by moment. Just like a river—flowing in and flowing out.

In this regard, never grieve the Holy Spirit. Ephesians 4:30 reads, "And do not grieve the Holy Spirit of God, by whom you were sealed for the day of redemption."

Never do a thing which will hinder His working in and through your life. Never criticize, judge, condemn, or talk about another Christian or any other Christian group. The very moment you begin to do or say something that He reminds you is wrong, stop it immediately. If you have offended either God or men, take immediate action to make things right.

Never quench the Holy Spirit. In 1 Th. 5:19 we read, "Do not quench the Spirit." Never say *No* to Him! As you

41

You can be a Soul Winner — Here's How!

walk through the day with the Lord, obey the Holy Spirit's every prompting. Always be sensitive to the whispers of this still, small voice. But remember, He speaks in accordance with His Word (1 Jn. 4:1).

5. *Continue to grow.*

The Spirit-filled life is not a status-quo experience. We must continue to follow the Lord (Lk. 9:23). And continue to seek Him for more (2 Pet. 3:18). And continue to walk in new truth that He shows us (1 Jn. 1:7).

D. End the day with the Lord.

Have a season of prayer the last thing each day. Ask the Lord to search your heart and to reveal anything done that day not in accordance with His will (Ps. 139:23-24). Take immediate action to correct anything which the Lord shows you. Never consider a day complete until you have the assurance that you are without offense toward God and toward men. Live your Christian life a day at a time. A wonderful fact to remember is this: If you live a victorious Christian life, a day at a time, you will in reality live a victorious Christian life all the time.

E. Additional suggestions.

As you continue to learn to walk in the Spirit, there are additional practices that we suggest you consider:

1. *Bible study.*

In addition to your morning Bible reading you should have a plan of Bible study. See Appendix J for various Bible study materials that are available. Also, there are some Bible study procedures suggested in Chapter 10.

2. *Scripture memorization.*

Many Christians today agree that Scripture memorization is one of the most personally profitable spiritual disciplines they have for the time involved. Great dividends are received for the few minutes invested each day. (The Bible study materials available in Appendix J include Scripture memory.)

EXPERIENCE THE SPIRIT-FILLED LIFE

3. *A journal.*

Buy a small hard-covered notebook and start a journal. Keep a record of the business you and the Lord transact. Enter lessons the Lord is teaching you. Enter Scripture passages that impress you and how the Lord is speaking to you through them. Keep a record of God's working in your life and in the lives of those for whom you are praying. Have the journal with you to make entries in your morning and evening times with the Lord.

4. *One-half day with the Lord monthly.*

In addition to your daily times and your daily walk with the Lord, you will find that spending one-half day monthly with the Lord can become one of the most profitable things you do.

a. With your Bible, journal, Bible studies, Scripture memory verses, and pen, go to a secluded spot where you can be alone with the Lord.

b. Begin with a time of prayer, asking His guidance and blessing.

c. Then review the verses you have memorized. Take your time. Meditate much as you go.

d. Then read your journal. Review how things have progressed since your last one-half day with the Lord a month earlier.

e. Follow this by slowly reading some favorite chapters in the Bible.

f. Then make an entry in your journal relative to your goals and personal projects for the coming month. Keep in mind your relationship with the Lord, to your family, to your job, and fellow employees, to your church and the work of the Lord, to your neighbors, your city, and the world.

You can be a Soul Winner—Here's How!

h. Conclude your time with a good season of prayer.

Ask the Lord to continue to mold you into a vessel that will glorify Him. And ask Him to continue making you useable—to evangelize the world and be a blessing to His people. Believe Him for great things (Jer. 33:3). Ask Him to do through you things beyond what you can even think (Eph. 3:20)!

Questions to Answer
1. What does the Holy Spirit do for every Christian?
2. What are the requirements for being filled with the Spirit?
3. What are the conditions for continuing the Spirit-filled life?

Questions for Meditation and Application
1. Does the Holy Spirit have His way in every area of your life?
2. How can you better discipline every area of your life in order to more perfectly and completely maintain a Spirit-controlled life?
3. Have you surrendered every area of your life to the Lord of the Harvest for the purpose of fulfilling the Great Commission? Do you want to see the gospel taken to every person in the world in this generation at any and all personal sacrifice?

Assignments
1. Begin to develop the habit of daily, morning devotions.
2. Give yourself to the Lord of the harvest for His use in His harvest. Ask God to use you to get the gospel to every person in the world in this generation.
3. Consider the suggestion made under Section E.

Chapter 3

Learn a Soul Winning Plan

Your third step in becoming an effective, Spirit-filled, personal soul winner is to learn a soul-winning plan.

I. WHY HAVE A SOUL-WINNING PLAN

A. Why we don't win more souls

Listed below are the major reasons why more Christians aren't effective personal soul winners. As you study this list, try to determine which of the reasons apply to your situation. Then you will know the areas you need to work on to become more effective for Jesus.

1. No concept or vision for this work.
2. Don't realize that the Lord wants to use you in this way.
3. Have the idea that it is a special *calling*.
4. Have the idea that one has to have the *gift*.
5. No one else does it.
6. Not spiritually prepared.
7. Not in touch or in contact with unsaved people.
8. Don't know how to approach or get next to unsaved people.
9. Don't know how to get started.
10. Don't know how to bring up the subject when with unsaved friends.
11. Don't know what Scripture to use when they show an interest in knowing the way of salvation.
12. Don't know how to bring the unsaved to a place of decision after you have witnessed and looked at the Bible together.
13. Fear.

You can be a Soul Winner — Here's How!

14. Have tried a soul-winning plan and it didn't work.

15. Have tried without a plan and failed, too.

16. Have the idea that one has to memorize dozens of Bible verses to be prepared.

17. Don't know how to answer all of the arguments, difficulties, and excuses which you think will occur.

18. Haven't set aside time specifically for soul winning.

B. The advantages of a soul-winning plan

The answer to the first five of the above reasons is found in a thorough study and wholehearted application of the truth and principles outlined in Chapter 1.

The answer to reason number six and a partial answer to many of the other reasons is found in Chapter 2. A major part of the answer to all of the other above reasons (7-18) is found in having a soul-winning plan.

By learning a soul-winning plan, anyone—even the most timid Christian—can begin to effectively and consistently bring people to Christ. Thousands of Christian people today— many of them having been a complete failure at soul winning for years—are regularly winning people to Christ. I wish you could meet some of them and hear them tell, in their own words, how wondrously God is using them.

By learning a soul-winning plan—

1. You will always be ready.

2. You will be able to guide the conversation from contact and normal conversation with the person right through to a place of decision with them. In this way you will be able to stay on target and bring the lost person to the Lord more simply and quickly than without a plan.

3. You are free of the stress of planning moves so that you can concentrate on the lost person and the Holy Spirit's presence and guidance.

4. You will gain confidence that results in boldness.

LEARN A SOUL WINNING PLAN

5. You will completely eliminate many arguments, difficulties, and excuses and answer most of the others before they ever come up.

C. Why these particular plans

In this chapter an attempt has been made to present a well-balanced, truly Biblical, practical, workable, realistic plan for presenting our wonderful Lord and His salvation to unsaved people just as presented in the Word of God.

It is a presentation of the Person of the Lord Jesus Christ rather than a plan of salvation or a set of verses since salvation is not basically in an experience but in a vital, personal relationship with Him.

There is a scriptural use of repentance, making it the doorway to saving faith, rather than leaving it out or over-emphasizing it. There is a presentation of the negative truths of sin, hell, judgment, and the wrath of God which is held in balance with the presentation of the positive truths of the love of God, the gift of eternal life, the joy, the peace, etc., again, as presented in Scripture.

They are plans which are practical. The original approach to personal soul winning, introduced by Mr. Torrey and Mr. Trumbull around 1900, required memorizing dozens of Scripture verses to deal with a person's every problem, difficulty, and excuse. This requirement of elaborate Scripture memorization made the approach impractical for use by the average pastor, to say nothing of the average believer. Additionally, it was easy for that approach to lead to a theological argument. Further, if this dealing with problems, difficulties, and excuses was successfully accomplished without an argument (which rarely happens), the soul winners still had a task of leading the seeker to the Lord Jesus. Personal soul-winning leaders since the 1950's have discovered that there is a more simple approach—an approach which eliminates problems, difficulties, and excuses. These are not the real problem anyway. The real problem is sin and its consequences. The real solution is a vital, personal relationship with the Lord Jesus Christ. And we all find Him basically the

47

You can be a Soul Winner—Here's How!

same way—by repentance and faith. The new approach, therefore, is simply a simple presentation of these basic gospel truths.

They are plans which assist the soul winner at the four most critical areas (which the old approach usually gave little help on)—(1) how to bring up the subject of spiritual things, (2) how to get into the Bible with your unsaved friend, (3) how to use the Word of God to effectively present Christ, and (4) how to bring your friend to a place of decision.

Scriptural terminology is used but explained in such a way as to be easily understood by the average non-Christian. The Lord's required discipleship is presented in proper balance with His saving power. And, finally, it is a plan which works—it has been used by the author and thousands of others on every continent in bringing many people of a wide variety of religious, educational, and social positions and backgrounds to the Lord Jesus Christ.

The soul-winning plans presented in this chapter consist of six steps—contact, transition, presentation, decision, assurance, and initial follow-up. They can be used with any person and in any situation appropriate for soul winning—in a home with an individual or a family, across the back fence with the neighbor, with someone seated beside you on the train, bus or plane, at a church altar, in an inquiry or counselor's room, at the jail, at a servicemen's center, in Sunday school, in a college dormitory or fraternity room, in the city park, at the bus, train, or plane terminal, in a hospital room—and on the list could go.

D. A marked New Testament or a witnessing booklet plan?

There are two basic types of soul-winning plans. Some people prefer to use a New Testament in their witnessing and soul winning. Others prefer some type of witnessing booklet. In this chapter you will be given both. No attempt is made to say which is better. Some people definitely prefer to use a Testament and others a booklet. We would suggest that you learn both. Then use the one with which you feel most comfortable.

48

LEARN A SOUL WINNING PLAN

To learn these plans we would suggest that you—

1. Read the entire chapter through once.
2. Study it in detail.
3. Modify the plans any way that you think makes them more suitable to you.
4. Memorize key points.
5. Practice on someone who will play the role of the unsaved person.
6. Begin to put the plans into action.
7. Alternate between in-the-field soul winning and further study of the plans until you have a plan of your own—either these or some modification of these that you have developed—that is part of your life.

In using these plans it is suggested that you avoid using Christian cliches and other terminology that unsaved persons might not understand. Present the truth, but do it in a way that will be understood by the person to whom you are witnessing.

II. A MARKED NEW TESTAMENT PLAN
A. An outline of the plan

1. *Contact*—meeting and talking with people.
2. *Transition*—using four questions to turn a contact into a soul-winning situation.
   a. "Have you ever thought much about spiritual things?"
   b. "Have you ever heard about knowing Jesus Christ in a vital, personal way?"
   c. "How would you say one comes to know Christ in this way?"
   d. "Would you like to look at six verses of Scripture that tell us about this?"
3. *Presentation*—presenting to your friend Jesus and His wonderful way of salvation.

You can be a Soul Winner—Here's How!

    a. Man's rebellion.

        1.) Rom. 3:23 - Man chose to go his own way—this attitude and act of rebellion is what the Bible calls sin—we are all guilty of this.

        2.) Rom. 6:23, part 1 - The consequences of sin— spiritual death, separation from God in this life and in the life to come.

    b. God's answer. Rom. 6:23, part 2 - The remedy—God loves us—wants to give us eternal life—a life of fellowship with God—in this life—and in the next—cannot work for it—through Jesus Christ. He's the Son of God—died for our sins—came back to life—lives today—can forgive and transform.

    c. Man's response.

        1.) Acts 3:19 - First thing we must do—repent—turn from our sins—sins blotted out.

        2.) Jn. 1:12 - Second thing we must do—personally receive Jesus Christ as Savior and Lord—difference between believing and receiving.

        3.) Rev. 3:20 - Jesus stands and knocks—if any man opens, He will come in.

4. *Decision*—drawing the net and leading your friend to Jesus.

    a. "What did you invite us to do?"

    b. "What should you invite Him to do?"

    c. "Do you know of any reason why you can't invite Jesus Christ into your life?"

    d. "Would you like to do this now?"

5. *Assurance*—helping your friend to have assurance of his salvation.

    a. Rev. 3:20 - Did he open the door? Did Christ come in?

    b. 1 Jn. 5:11-12 - What does he have?

LEARN A SOUL WINNING PLAN

6. *Initial follow-up*—help your friend to begin to get established.

    a. Leave information for new Christians.

    b. Get him started in daily devotions.

    c. Encourage him to tell someone.

    d. Arrange to see him again in two days.

    e. A *thank you* prayer.

B. The plan in operation

1. *Contact.* The first step in your soul-winning plan is the contact. You can't lead anyone to the Lord, you can't even witness to them, until you're in contact with them. It is this contact that prepares the way for soul winning. This is therefore, the soul winner's first goal, and includes meeting the person, getting acquainted, and winning their friendship and confidence. It may take 15 minutes. For example:

   - Someone you walk to school with
   - You're sitting next to someone on the plane
   - You meet someone in the park
   - You're sitting next to someone on a bench waiting for a city bus
   - You go to call in a home of a couple who recently visited your church or who your church located through some type of survey

   In these cases, you introduce yourself, strike up a conversation, and get acquainted. Or it may take longer—an hour, a month, a year, much of a life-time. Examples:

   - Your neighbors
   - The fellow you work beside
   - Your relatives
   - Your boss
   - Some very distinguished folks in your city

51

You can be a Soul Winner — Here's How!

But in all cases, the preparation work is extremely important. And it's easy to do. Much of it consists of simply meeting and talking with people. It is something that you do everyday. And it is these simple, everyday contacts that can be turned into opportunities for the Lord.

2. *Transition.* The second step in your personal soul-winning plan is the transition. This is where you turn this everyday contact into a soul-winning situation.

One of the big reasons why most people have never led a soul to Christ is because they have never known how to bring up the subject, or they have used a blunt approach like "Are you saved?" and have met with failure. With the transition you bring up the subject of spiritual things and progress gently and slowly, yet definitely and successfully, right to the place where they willingly consent to look at what the Bible says. This is the second major goal of the soul winner —to get into the Bible.

With the transition—

a. You bridge the gap from normal conversation with a person to presenting the Lord Jesus Christ to him.

b. You help him feel at ease discussing spiritual things with you.

c. You find out, unknown to him, his spiritual condition. As he talks, ask yourself

1) What does he know?

2) What are his needs?

3) What response has he already made?

The transition is made with the use of four questions. Regardless of their response to each question, you can make an appropriate comment and go on to the next question.

You do not have to ask these questions *word perfect*, but you should commit them to memory for ease of use at first.

52

LEARN A SOUL WINNING PLAN

- "(Name), have you ever thought much about spiritual things?"
- "Have you ever heard about knowing Jesus Christ in a vital, personal way?"
- "How would you say one comes to know Christ in this way?"
- "Would you like to look at five verses of Scripture that tell us about this?"

Notice the progression here—spiritual things, knowing Christ, how to know him, can we look in the Bible. Notice also that it is never made personal, such as, "Do you know Christ?" That's too pointed. It would build barriers. Making it impersonal actually tears down barriers.

There will be cases where you will have to reword the questions some. For instance—if you ask the first question, "(Name), have you ever thought much about spiritual things?"

And he says, "No!"

Then you would reword the second question, "I don't suppose then that you have ever heard about knowing Jesus Christ in a vital, personal way?"

Then go directly to the last question.

In going through the transition, remember that it is God's responsibility to open the doors. It's our job to walk through the doors that He opens. These four questions are a way that you can get started—and keep going as long as the doors continue to open. When you run into a door that is definitely closed—stop; don't try to force it open. Back off, pray, wait, give the Holy Spirit time to work. Then go back when the Spirit tells you to. So the transition is a way to get started.

Now let's see this transition in operation. Let's say that you're calling in the home of a family who have recently visited your church. You proceed to get acquainted as

53

You can be a Soul Winner — Here's How!

outlined in Chapter 4. Now the time has come to get down to business. You proceed. (The bold portion is the soul winner's conversation.)

"It was certainly good to see you folks in church a few Sundays ago. (pause) I suppose you've thought quite a lot about spiritual things?"

"Oh, yes, we try to get to church as often as we can."

"Have you ever heard about knowing Jesus Christ in a vital personal way, Mr. Smith?"

"Yes, I went to Sunday school when I was a boy in Iowa."

"And, Mrs. Smith?"

"I'm not sure."

"How would you say one comes to know Christ in this way?"

Mr. Smith says, "Boy, you got me there!"

And she says, "To be baptized, I think."

The soul winner says, **"I see. (pause) "Would you like to look at five verses of Scripture that tell about this?"**

The response to this question will almost always be, "Sure, that would be fine."

The author has found that most people, if approached properly, as explained here, want to see what the Bible says. Let's face it—people are hungry.

The average person world-wide today is *uptight*. All of us are being pressured from many directions—the possibility of nuclear warfare, terrorism, economic insecurity, famine, running out of clean air and water, family problems, and on the list could go. Because of this, people world-wide are looking for answers.

After the transition, you are now ready to proceed with the presentation.

3. *Presentation.* Presentation, the third step in your soul-winning plan, consists of presenting to your friend the most wonderful Person in the world—God—and His

LEARN A SOUL WINNING PLAN

marvelous salvation through Jesus Christ. To do this you will use six verses of Scripture—Rom. 3:23, 6:23; Acts 3:19; Jn. 1:12; Rev. 3:20, and 1 Jn. 5:11-12.

As the lost person responds favorably to looking at the Bible, you will take out your marked New Testament, which should be concealed until your unsaved friend consents to look at the Bible with you. The sight of a Bible previous to this can cause harmful barriers on his part (Prov. 1:17).

Verse 1, Rom. 3:23: **"This first verse tells us why we need to come to know Jesus Christ. Here, (name), why don't you read this verse aloud for us."**

Hold your Testament for him to read aloud.

"For all have sinned and fall short of the glory of God."

"What does God say that we have all done?"

"We have all sinned."

"Yes, (name), we have ALL SINNED. Every person that has ever lived, except Jesus Christ, has sinned. Do you have any idea what it means to sin?"

His response will be something like "Well, I suppose it's when we do something wrong."

You should make an appropriate comment to his response, such as, **"That certainly hits the nail on the head."** Or, **"Yes, that's right."**

And then make an accurate definition of sin as follows: **"God is the author of laws and commandments by which He governs the universe. Some of these are physical, like the law of gravity. Others are spiritual. The heart of God's spiritual laws are the Ten Commandments. When we willfully break His spiritual laws or disobey these Commandments, we sin** (1 Jn. 3:4).

"Let's consider the Ten Commandments. It says that we should not kill, not commit adultery, not steal, not covet, not lie, not use God's name in vain, not worship

You can be a Soul Winner—Here's How!

idols. It says that we should love our parents and remember the Sabbath. And that we should have no other gods before Him; He should be the most important thing in our lives; we should love Him with all our hearts.

"But instead of loving God with all of our hearts, we have chosen to go our own way—to run our own lives—to break His laws—to disobey His Commandments—to try to work things out for ourselves rather than yielding our lives to God.

"It's amazing how unimportant most of us consider the practice of sin to be. We see everyone doing these things that are wrong, so we feel that we are not so bad off. But this is not the case. God is holy and righteous. He hates sin, and He says that one sin will destroy our souls. And we only have to break one of these commandments one time to stand before God guilty" (Jas. 2:10).

(Pause to give the Holy Spirit time to do His convicting work.)

Your friend will not be interested in getting saved until the Holy Spirit reveals to him that he is lost. It is also important that you never tell a person he is a sinner, or tell him what his sins are (who are we to know anyway!), or try to convict him, or piously look down on him. It is the Holy Spirit's job to convict your friend of his sin (Jn. 16:8). You share Rom. 3:23 with him, define sin, and leave the rest to the Holy Spirit. Be assured that He will make it personal to your friend. For instance, when you mention "Thou shalt not take the Lord's name in vain," at that instant the Holy Spirit will remind your friend of all the times that he has used God's name in vain. Remember to take your time to give the Spirit a chance to work.

"When we look at it this way, it's easy to see why the Bible can say that we all have sinned, isn't it?"

His response may be something like "Yes, it certainly is. I know that I have sinned."

56

LEARN A SOUL WINNING PLAN

Now make the transition to the next verse by making appropriate comment to his response and by stating the purpose of the first part of the next verse as you turn to Rom. 6:23.

Verse 2, part 1: "Yes, (name), we all have sinned. And not only have we sinned, but sin has a consequence. The first part of this next verse tells us the CONSE-QUENCES OF OUR SINS."

Once again let your unsaved friend read from your Testament.

"For the wages of sin is death."

"Here we find the Bible talks about a wage. A wage, you know, (name), is something we have earned, or deserve, or have coming. When we work, we expect to get paid exactly what we have earned or deserve. Right?"

"Right."

"Here we see that our sin has earned us a wage. What is that wage?"

Let him look at the Testament again until he sees the answer and says, "Death."

"Yes, the wages we deserve, or have coming, because of our sin is death. This death is more than just physical death—it is spiritual death and means separation from God."

(Pause to give the Spirit a chance to drive this truth home.)

"We are separated from God two ways. First, because of our sin, we are separated from God's fellowship in this life. Adam and Eve in the garden of Eden had fellow-ship with God, they knew God, they talked intimately with Him. We don't have that kind of fellowship with God today, do we?"

"No, we certainly don't."

57

You can be a Soul Winner—Here's How!

"And this is the real source of all our problems, fears, frustrations, and lack of peace of mind—we're not in touch with God. We've lost personal contact with the One who made us."

(Pause for the Spirit to work.)

"And then there is a second way in which we are separated from God. Because of our sin we will be separated from God's presence forever in the place Jesus called "hell" in the next life. I know, (name), that these are days when we don't hear much about hell and when most people say they don't believe in such a place. But the Bible has much to say about hell. And Jesus Christ Himself said more about hell than He did about heaven."

(Pause)

"The Bible doesn't present a very good picture for us, does it?"

His response will probably be, "No, it sure doesn't. I've never thought of it quite this way."

Verse 2, part 2: Now make the transition to the second part of this third verse with, **"But there's another side to this picture, (name), and how thankful we can be. God loves us. And He has provided a way that we can come back into fellowship with Him. Let's look at the second part of this verse."**

Again, hold the Testament for him to read aloud.

"But the free gift of God is eternal life in Christ Jesus our Lord."

"God wants to give us a gift. And what is this gift?"

"Eternal life."

"Yes, God wants to give us eternal life as a free gift. Eternal life is a life of fellowship with God. God has provided a way that we can come back into fellowship with Him in this life—and go to be with Him forever in the life to come. That's quite a gift, isn't it?"

LEARN A SOUL WINNING PLAN

"It sure is!"

"You notice that it is a 'free gift'. Can we work for it?"

Pause for his response. He will probably say, "No, it wouldn't be a gift then."

If he doesn't make this response, proceed to help him understand with, **"No, we cannot work for it because then it would not be a gift."**

(Pause)

"There are many people today who think that they will go to heaven if they simply live a good moral life, pay their debts, and do the best they can. But these things, as well as church membership and baptism, will not get us to heaven. We cannot earn eternal life. We must simply receive it as a free gift."

(Pause)

"You see there are two ways in which we can respond to this gift which God offers to us. To illustrate, let me offer you this pen (take your pen from your pocket and offer it to your friend) **as a free gift. What are the two ways in which you can respond to my offer?"**

His response will probably be, "I can take it or refuse it."

If he doesn't make this response, help him to understand this point by saying, **"You can receive it or refuse it, can't you?"**

Once this point has been clearly seen proceed with, **"And this is the way it is with eternal life, (name). God offers it to us as a free gift. We can refuse it or we can simply receive it. The choice is up to us."**

(Pause)

"Now let's see who the gift of eternal life is through."

Again let him see the Testament. His response will probably be, "Through Jesus Christ."

"Yes, the gift of eternal life is through Jesus Christ. Do you know why it is through Jesus Christ, (name)?"

59

You can be a Soul Winner — Here's How!

His response will be varied at this point, such as, "Well, He died for us." Or, "Well, He's the Son of God." Or, "No, I really don't know."

Regardless of his response you should make an appropriate comment and explain, **"The gift of eternal life is through Jesus Christ because of, first, who He is; second, what He did 2000 years ago; and third, what He can do for us today."**

(Pause)

"First, (name), Who is He?"

He will make some response like, "He's the Son of God." Or, "He's the Savior." Or, "He was a good man."

Regardless of his response, you make an appropriate comment and tell Who He is, **"Yes, (name), He's the Son of God. He is God's perfect revelation of Himself to sinful mankind. He's the proof of God's love for us. Sinful man could not reach up and find God, so God reached down to man in the person of Jesus Christ. Isn't that wonderful?"**

Wait for his response. Then go on.

(Note: If they doubt any of this and sincerely need further proof of these truths, you may show them Jn. 3:16. These cases, however, will be few.)

"Now let's consider what He did for us 2000 years ago."

(Pause)

"What did He do?"

Give him a chance to respond. Make an appropriate comment to his response and proceed with, **"He died for our sins—every sin you and I have ever committed—on the cross almost 2000 years ago. This wage or consequence which we deserve for our sins which we talked about earlier, Jesus Christ paid it. He shed His blood to take away our sins. He took the consequences of our sins upon Himself on the cross."**

(Pause)

LEARN A SOUL WINNING PLAN

"Then what else did Jesus Christ do?"

Let him respond, make an appropriate comment, and proceed with, **"He arose from the dead. (Pause) He came back to life (pause) and He lives today. (Pause) And because Jesus Christ lives today, (name), He can do some things for us that no one else can do. (Pause) He can forgive us for all of our sins—no one else can do that, except Jesus Christ."**

(Pause)

"Not only can He forgive our past sins, but Jesus Christ has the power to transform us and to make us the kind of people He wants us to be. He can actually invade our hearts and our lives, and by His Divine power, free us from the power of sin, give us power to resist temptation, and permit us to live a wonderful life of fellowship with Him."

(Pause)

"And with this transformation comes forgiveness, joy, peace of mind, new attitudes, and new purpose in life."

(Pause)

"Sounds wonderful, doesn't it—forgiveness, peace, joy, purpose, and some day heaven?"

Verse 3: His response will be varied at this point, but you can make an appropriate comment and, as you turn to Acts 3:19, make the transition to the third verse.

"Now let's look at what we have to do to receive all of this. What do we read here?"

Again let him read from your Testament.

"Repent therefore, and return, that your sins may be wiped away, in order that times of refreshing may come from the presence of the Lord."

"Here we see that the first thing we must do to receive all of this is to repent. Do you know what this word *repent* means?"

61

You can be a Soul Winner—Here's How!

His response will be varied at this point but you can make an appropriate comment and proceed with, *"Repent means to be truly sorry for our sins! This involves recognizing our life of sin, being sorry for it, coming humbly as a sinner to God, asking Him to forgive, and turning away from our life of sin, and turning to God."*

(Pause)

"And what does God say He will do to our sins when we repent?"

His response will probably be, "He will blot them out."

"Yes, (name), when we turn from our sins to God, our sins are blotted out—God forgives—it's as if we had never sinned. Sounds wonderful, doesn't it?"

Verse 4: As you turn to Jn. 1:12, make the transition to this fifth verse with, **"Now, let's look at the second thing we must do to receive this wonderful gift of eternal life."**

Again hold the Testament so he can read.

"But as many as received Him, to them gave He power to become children of God."

"We're not all children of God, are we?"

His response will probably be, "No, just those that receive Him."

"That's right, and the second thing we must do to receive this wonderful gift of eternal life is to personally receive Jesus Christ."

(Pause)

"It's very important at this point to understand that there's a big difference between believing and receiving. (Pause) Again let's illustrate with the pen. I'll offer it to you as a free gift. You believe I'm offering it, don't you?"

"Sure."

"But do you have it?"

"No."

62

LEARN A SOUL WINNING PLAN

"Why not?"

"Because I haven't taken it."

"That's exactly right. And this is the way it is with receiving Jesus Christ. It is not enough to believe in Jesus Christ. (Pause) There are many, many people today who believe in Christ. They believe He was born of a virgin, they believe He was the Son of God, they believe He is the Savior of the world, and so forth; but they have never personally received Him. They have never reached out and taken Him into their lives by personal invitation." (Pause) "We must receive Him as our Savior and Lord. We must receive Him as our Savior. This means we confess our sins to Him and ask His forgiveness. This means that we put all of our hope for salvation in Jesus—not in what we can do, or in any church, or preacher or priest—but in Jesus alone. We put all of our trust in Him. And we must receive Him as our Lord. We must turn our whole self over to Him— for Him to make of us and our lives what he wants. He becomes our Lord, our Master."

Briefly Review: "So, we've all sinned; our sin has terrible consequences in this life and in the next; but God loves us and wants to give us eternal life as a free gift; if we will turn from our sins and personally receive Jesus Christ as our Savior and Lord."

Verse 5: Turn to Rev. 3:20 and explain, "This is Jesus talking here."

Again let him read the Testament.

"Behold, I stand at the door and knock; if any one hears my voice and opens the door, I will come in to him, and will dine with him, and he with Me."

(Pause)

"Here Jesus is talking about the door of our heart and life. (Pause) He says that He stands at this door and knocks. (Pause) And if any man, any one of us, will

You can be a Soul Winner—Here's How!

hear His voice and will open the door of our heart and life, what does He promise to do?"

"He says that He will come in."

"Yes, (name), if we will open the door of our heart and life, Jesus Christ promises that He will come in. And what else will He do?"

"He will dine with us."

"Yes, (name), He will have fellowship with us, like when you sit around the dining table and have fellowship with your best friend. We will be back in fellowship with God like we were made to be. Doesn't that sound wonderful, (name)?"

You have just presented the Lord Jesus Christ to your unsaved friend. You are now ready to help him respond to the knocking Savior. Do not stop at this point. Let the Holy Spirit use you to lead him into a vital, personal relationship with the Savior.

4. *Decision.* The fourth step in your personal soul winning plan is to DRAW THE NET—help the lost person see that he must respond to the knocking Savior, and BRING HIM TO THE SAVIOR. This is done with four definite questions.

   Proceed with, **"Let's illustrate the truth of this verse this way. When we came to your home this evening, we wanted to come in, so we knocked on the door."**

   (Pause)

   a. **"And what did you invite us to do?"**

      (Or it may be more appropriate for instance, if you're riding together on the train or are any place other than a home to say, **"If your best friend should come to your home, and he knocked on the door, what would you tell him to do?"**)

      "Come in, of course."

LEARN A SOUL WINNING PLAN

"Sure, (name), and Jesus Christ, the best friend you'll ever have, likewise, stands knocking at the door of your heart right now."

(Pause)

b. **"What should you invite Him to do?"**

"Come in."

"Yes, you should invite Him to come in."

(Pause)

"I did this (number) years ago, and it's been the best thing I've ever done."

At this point you may want to take a minute to give a little of your own testimony. Or have your partner give his. There's power in this (Rev. 12:11). Tell (1) what your life was like before you met Christ, (2) how you found the Lord, and (3) what He has done for you and meant to you since. See Section IV of this chapter for more on this. Then proceed with,

c. **"Now, (name), do you know of any reason why you can't invite Jesus Christ into your life?"**

At this point he may ask honest questions, have some real problems, or bring up some excuse. If there is an honest question or a real problem, this is the time for you to deal with it. See Chapter 9 for how to handle excuses. And, of course, he or she may not be ready to turn his/her life over to the Lord. This, too, is dealt with in Chapter 9. This third question will also help you to see whether or not the fruit is *ripe* and *ready* to *pick*. If it is not ripe you would back off as explained in Chapter 9. In most situations, however, he will be ready to turn to the Lord. His response to question 3 will be something like this,

"No, I can't think of any."

You will proceed with, **"Wonderful, (name)! Remember what is involved. This means that you are turning from all in your life that you know is**

65

You can be a Soul Winner—Here's How!

displeasing to God, and without reservation you are turning your life over to Jesus Christ. (Pause) **This is not something we do today and forget tomorrow. This is the most important step you'll ever take."**

(Pause)

d. **"Would you like to do this right now, (name)? We can have prayer together. I'll pray first and then you can talk to the Lord. You can tell Him about your sin, ask His forgiveness, open the door of your heart, and invite Him to come in and take over your life. Okay?"**

At this point he may try to put the Lord off. If this is the case, proceed as outlined in Chapter 9. But generally his response will be, "Yes, I know I need to do this."

"Wonderful, (name), let's pray."

Then you immediately bow your head, close your eyes, and begin to pray.

"Dear Lord Jesus, thank You for coming into my heart and life (number) years ago. You have been so wonderful and good to me since then. Thank You tonight for this privilege of meeting and talking with (name) about You. He realizes that he is a sinner but that You died for his sin. Today he wants to turn from his sin and invite You into his heart. Please forgive him and save him now as he talks to You."

Then, with your head still bowed, say to your friend, **"Now, (name), you talk to the Lord Jesus. In your own words, tell Him about your sin, ask His forgiveness and invite Him to come into your heart and life."**

At this point two things may happen—he may go ahead and pray, or he may hesitate and indicate that he needs help in praying. If he goes ahead and prays, he may pray a general prayer or he may pray a spe-

LEARN A SOUL WINNING PLAN

cific prayer for salvation. If he prays a general prayer or if he indicates the need for help in praying, you should assist him by suggesting he repeat after you as you lead in short phrases something as follows: **"Dear Lord Jesus—I know I am a sinner—but You died on the cross for my sins—I need You as my personal Savior—and right now—I turn from my sin—and take You as my Savior—and I open my heart to You—I invite You to come in—I turn my life over to You—I make You my Lord—please forgive me and save me—make me the kind of person You want me to be—Amen."**

In every situation where the lost person indicates that he is ready to become a Christian, you (1) pray and then (2) make sure that he prays a specific prayer of salvation.

When you pray, try to pray in your own natural language if possible rather than in a *King James* language. This will help him see that prayer is simply talking to God in your own words. For more information on the art of praying in everyday language we strongly recommend the book *Prayer, Conversing with God* by Rosalind Rinker. Some have asked about the position of praying. You should assume the position of prayer which is most natural to them. They may indicate this by a motion to stand or kneel. If not, pray in your present, seated position.

You have drawn the net and helped your unsaved person meet Jesus as his Lord and Savior. Wonderful! You are now ready to help this new-born Christian have the assurance of his salvation.

5. *Assurance.* Assurance, the fifth step in your personal soul-winning plan, consists of helping the new-born Christian to have assurance of his salvation. You cannot give them this assurance. This is the Holy Spirit's job (Rom. 8:16). He may do it then or it may happen later. (And of course it won't happen at all if they haven't really meant busi-

You can be a Soul Winner—Here's How!

ness with the Lord.) But usually the Holy Spirit will give the assurance then, and do it through the Word (Eph. 6:17). After the lost person's prayer for salvation, proceed with, **"Now, (name), this may sound like a strange question, but did you really mean what you just prayed? Did you open the door of your heart to the Lord?"**

"Sure."

Now show him Rev. 3:20 again and ask, **"And what did the Lord Jesus say He would do if you opened the door?"**

"He said He would come in."

"Did He?"

"Yes, He must have; I feel so wonderful!"

Make sure that the new-born Christian is convinced in his heart (1) that he did open the door and (2) that Christ is in his heart. Then, as you turn to 1 Jn. 5:11-12, proceed with, **"Now let's look at one last passage of Scripture."**

<u>Verse 6</u>: He or she will read, "And the witness is this, that God has given us eternal life, and this life is in His Son. He who has the Son has the life; he who does not have the Son of God, does not have life."

"You notice that the Bible is talking about a special kind of life here. What is that life?"

"Eternal life."

"Yes, eternal life. And it says that if we have the Son, we have eternal life. Right?"

"Yes."

"Who is the Son?"

"Jesus Christ, of course."

"Do you have the Son?"

"Yes."

"Where do you have Him?"

"In my heart."

LEARN A SOUL WINNING PLAN

"Then do you have eternal life?"

"Yes, I do."

"Isn't that wonderful. Think of it, (name). You have eternal life right now. Your sins are forgiven. You have become a child of God. Now God can begin to work out His wonderful plan for your life."

As soon as your friend has the assurance that he is saved, you are ready to proceed to the sixth and last step in your personal soul-winning plan.

6. *Initial Follow-Up.* Initial follow-up, the sixth and last step in your personal soul-winning plan, consists of (1) leaving appropriate instructions with the new-born Christian to help him in the early days of his Christian life, and (2) making specific arrangements to see him again within two days.

   Five things are involved.

   a. One of the most effective ways to help him in the early days of his Christian life is to leave with him a tract or small brochure written especially for young Christians. This brochure should emphasize the importance of daily Bible reading and prayer, witnessing, and Christian fellowship.

   b. Based on instructions in the leaflet or booklet, make a specific suggestion that the new Christian begin the very next day to spend 15 minutes in morning devotions reading a chapter in the Bible each day and talking with the Lord. The author likes to suggest 1 Jn. as a starter. It deals with basic issues—sin, forgiveness, God's love, our love to God and our fellowman, Satan, prayer, victory, etc. It is only five chapters long so, at the rate of one chapter a day, he will finish it in five days with a real sense of accomplishment. Others suggest starting in the Gospel of John or Mark. Do not leave until he has agreed to spend 15 minutes the next morning in the Bible and prayer.

You can be a Soul Winner—Here's How!

    c. Again based on instructions given in the booklets, suggest to your newly saved friend that he tell someone what he has done the first chance he has and before that day is over, if possible (Mt. 10:32-33; Rom.10:9-10).

    d. Then make specific arrangements to see him again in two or three days

        1) To see how his daily devotions are coming

        2) To see if he has questions

        3) To encourage him, and

        4) To have prayer with him.

    e. Just before you leave, close your time together with a *thank you* prayer. This time let him pray first. Proceed with, **"Before I leave, (name), let's talk to the Lord Jesus once more. This time you lead us in prayer and thank Him for what He has done for you today."** After he has prayed, you should pray and then graciously and joyously depart.

    The initial follow-up is now completed, but your job has just begun. This is just the beginning of the complete task of follow-up. You are this new-born Christian's spiritual father (or mother). You will want to continue to work with him until he is a mature, Spirit-filled, soul-winning Christian like yourself. For further suggestions on this task, see Chapters 10 and 11.

III. WITNESSING BOOKLET PLANS

Another excellent approach to personal evangelism is with the use of some type of witnessing booklet. This concept was introduced in the mid 1960s with Campus Crusade's *Four Spiritual Laws* booklet. Since that time many more have been published. We have one entitled *The Way to God*—see Appendix J for further information.

LEARN A SOUL WINNING PLAN

A. Contact

The contact step would be similar as with the Testament approach. However, the booklet can also be used as a door-opener in door-to-door work. See Chapter 6 for further details.

B. Transition

The transition with the witnessing booklet also is similar to the Testament approach except that the fourth question should be changed to something like, **"May I share with you this little booklet that tells how one can come to know Jesus Christ?"**

You actually can use the booklet's title in your fourth question. For instance if you are using *The Way to God* you might say, **"May I share with you this little booklet that tells how one can find his way to God?"**

C. Presentation

When you get to the actual presentation of the gospel, let the person read the first section of the booklet (usually the first two pages) aloud. Then answer any questions they may ask or make any additional comments that you feel led to make. You can, of course, just read through the booklet with your friend without making any comments. After finishing the first section, proceed on to the second section (usually the next two pages).

If you are talking to more than one person at the same time, such as a family in their home, give a copy of the booklet to each person. Suggest that the husband read the first section. Then the wife might read the second. Then someone else the third section, etc.

D. Decision

With the booklet approach there usually is an actual prayer printed in the booklet that you can pray with your unsaved friend if they are ready to repent of their sins and turn to the Lord Jesus.

71

You can be a Soul Winner — Here's How!

E. Assurance

With the booklet approach there also is usually an assurance section that you can discuss with them after they have turned their life over to the Lord Jesus Christ.

F. Initial follow-up

With the booklet approach there usually is a page at the end of the booklet that gives helpful suggestions to the new Christian that you can discuss with your friend by way of initial follow-up. Be sure to make an appointment to see him again in a few days. Also be sure to give him opportunity to pray a prayer of thanks before you part.

This type of booklet can also be used as a give-away piece of literature. In this case, you would not sit down and read and discuss it with your friend, but would simply give it to them to read at their own leisure.

IV. HOW TO GIVE YOUR PERSONAL TESTIMONY

In Acts 26:1-29, Paul told King Agrippa the story of his conversion. He first told what his life was like before he met Jesus in verses 4-11. In verses 12-18 he tells of his conversion. In verses 19-23 he tells what his life has been like since.

Giving your testimony, likewise, is a very effective way to witness. Take some time, sit down, and write out your story. Make it about three pages in length. Page one should be about your life before you met Jesus. On page two tell how you met Jesus. On page three tell how your life has been since then. Practice sharing this with some Christian friend. Then trust the Lord for opportunities where you can begin sharing it with unsaved people. God will use your story to point people to Jesus Christ.

V. OTHER SOUL WINNING METHODS

There are many other approaches to personal evangelism—flip charts, video presentations of the gospel, audio tape presentations, etc. Try whatever you feel comfortable with. Let God show you His infinite variety of ways to reach your unsaved friends.

LEARN A SOUL WINNING PLAN

Questions to Answer

1. Why have a soul-winning plan?
2. What are the six steps of the soul-winning plan presented in this chapter?
3. What are the six verses used in the Testament soul-winning plan?

Questions for Meditation and Application

1. Considering the reasons given in the first part of the chapter, why haven't you been a more effective soul winner in the past? What do you plan to do to improve the situation?
2. Do you think the six verses with their explanations used in the plan in this chapter cover all that one basically needs to know to be saved?
3. How do you need to change the plans given in this chapter to more closely fit your personality?
4. How can you most quickly and effectively learn a soul-winning plan?

Assignment

1. Learn a soul-winning plan.

You can be a Soul Winner—Here's How!

Chapter 4

Learn a Home Visitation Procedure

Much of the evangelism work of the First Century was done in homes (Mt. 10:12; Mk. 5:19; Lk. 7:36-50; Acts 5:42, 11:12, 20:20). Likewise, calling on an individual or family in their home presents one of the most opportune and effective situations for witnessing and soul winning today. It is here that they are relaxed. It is here that they have time to think and to talk. Besides, if you evangelize the homes of a city, you automatically evangelize a city because everybody has a place they call home. Even those in the hospital and jail will someday be home. You will also know where to come to see them again for effective follow-up work.

Your next step, therefore, in becoming an effective Spirit-filled, soul winner is to learn how to visit in a home. By learning this procedure you will be able to call at any home in the community and set the stage for soul winning. The author knows of churches that are using these procedures to knock on every door in their community. They are seeing results! For information on how a group of churches in a city can cooperatively evangelize their city, see Appendix G—Reaching Cities for Christ.

Some of the details of this chapter will have to be adjusted to the situation. For instance, you will obviously not have to introduce yourselves at the door if you are already acquainted. The chapter is written to be all-inclusive and assumes you are going to call in a new home.

I. ADVANCED PREPARATION

A. Locate and pray for prospects

Make contacts and locate prospects as outlined in Chapter 6. Take five families (or individuals if you're working on a college campus, for instance) for your personal responsibility and begin to pray for them daily as outlined in Chapter 7.

75

You can be a Soul Winner — Here's How!

Some of your soul-winning work in homes will be with these for whom you feel personally responsible. Other home visitation work will be with prospects your church has located, some of which you have never met before.

There are times when it is best to make an appointment a day or two in advance of your visit. For example, you want to talk with a fellow employee and his family, or you want to talk with an unsaved family who have recently started attending your church. In other cases, you should not make an appointment in advance. For example, a family located through a census. A general practice would be: consider making an appointment if you are already acquainted and know that they would appreciate a visit with reference to spiritual things. If you're not sure how open they are, don't make an appointment—just go!

There may be times when it will be best to make an appointment with a family for a time after the children are in bed if they are all quite small. Also, there will be a few cases where it is best for the soul winner to go alone to a particular home, such as a situation where the person or family are very open to the soul winner and might not be as open if someone else were along.

B. Prepare spiritually

Although you should always be ready spiritually to witness and to win souls, you should be especially so before you go with that express purpose. Reread Chapter 2 and ask the Lord to speak to you through it. Have a light meal the evening of calling and spend as much time as possible in fasting and prayer (see Chapter 7).

C. Proper grooming

Proper grooming is very important to soul winning. God looks at the heart, but man looks at the outward appearance (1 Sam. 16:7). So dress neatly, make sure that your fingernails are properly cleaned and trimmed, your hair neatly combed, your shoes shined, your breath sweet, etc. How much you dress-up will depend upon who you are going to see. You

LEARN A HOME VISITATION PROCEDURE

would obviously dress different to visit a poor family in the inner-city ghetto than a wealthy family in the suburbs. Remember, you're an ambassador for Jesus Christ (2 Cor. 5:20).

II. JUST BEFORE THE VISIT

A. Check your materials

Make sure that you have your marked New Testament, witnessing booklets and gospel leaflets, initial follow-up material, blank prospect cards, church information, a flashlight, and a city map (see Chapter 5).

B. Decide on the soul winner

The best way to go witnessing is in teams of two. Jesus sent the Twelve (Lk. 9) and Seventy (Lk. 10) out this way. You both have an important role to play. One of you will be the leader of the team and do the actual soul winning. The other will baby-sit, pray, and learn by observing. We have occasionally sent people in teams of three. For instance, we've had teenagers who wanted to go out and they didn't have any teens that they knew to go to, so we would pair two teens with one adult and send them out to witness to families. Or sometimes, we had an extra person with nobody to pair them with and have sent out a team of three. Generally, however, teams of two are better.

You need to decide ahead of time who's going to be the leader and who's going to be the silent partner. In many cases, one will be more experienced than the other. The more experienced would be the leader and the less experienced will go along as a silent partner. One of the purposes of going along is to learn. The silent partner does three things: baby-sits, prays, and learns by watching. Now if it's a husband and wife team going out together, unless you are talking to a lady the husband should be the leader.

C. Have prayer together

Have a good season of prayer together in your car before starting out for the home. Ask God to give you open doors

77

You can be a Soul Winner—Here's How!

(Col. 4:3), wisdom (Jas. 1:5), and boldness (Acts 4:29). And ask Him to open hearts (Acts 16:14), convict of sin (Jn. 16:8), reveal His Son (Jn. 15:26), and save (2 Pet. 3:9) those to whom you are going.

D. Memorize their name

As you drive toward their home, memorize the family's name, mention to each other any other things necessary for the visit, and pray silently. Do not talk about other subjects.

E. Approach the home quietly and observantly

Do not talk as you leave your car and approach the family's home. Walk on their sidewalk. Learn all that you can about them by observing the yard and the porch. For example, if there's a tricycle on the porch you'll know that they have small children. Knock or ring the doorbell, step back a step, and wait for someone to answer.

III. AT THE DOOR

A. The greeting

As someone answers the door, begin your conversation with a greeting—"Hello, Hi, How do you do, Howdy, Good evening, etc."—whatever is natural for you. Be sure to start with the greeting. And be sure to be yourself.

B. The Introduction

Next comes the introduction and an explanation of where you are from. You're not there to talk to them about the church. You're there to talk to them about the Lord. But they need to know if you are Jehovah's Witnesses, or Fuller Brush Salesmen, or the FBI, so inform them:

"My name is Jack Jones and this is Bill Smith. We are from The Community Church on the corner of Maple and First."

Be genuinely friendly and loving. Smile. Let the joy of the Lord be seen through you.

C. Explain your purpose for being there

Then explain your purpose for being at the home. The three most popular approaches at the door are: giving away free

LEARN A HOME VISITATION PROCEDURE

Christian literature, a visit from the church, or a religious survey.

If your approach is a visit from the church, you would proceed with something like this:

"We're so glad that Johnny comes to Sunday school. And we're out in the neighborhood this evening, getting acquainted with folks. We thought if you folks had a few minutes, we'd like to get acquainted with you."

The details of each of the other approaches is given in Chapter 6. Regardless of the approach you used, go as far with the family as you can. At some homes you will be invited in.

D. Special situations that may develop

1. *If a woman answers.* If two men or a husband and wife team are out together, and a lady answers the door, you will want to make sure that the husband is home before going in. Two men should not visit a lady alone for obvious reasons—the temptation of immorality, what the neighbors might say, how the husband might react. A husband and wife team could call on a woman without her husband being there, but they would have to return later to talk with the husband. So a better use of time would be to wait and talk with both husband and wife at a later time.

2. *If a child answers.* If a child answers the door, ask to speak with one of the parents. Do not enter the home at the child's invitation. The parent may not want you in the house. If you enter at the child's invitation, he will "get in trouble" when you leave. So wait for the parent to come and invite you into the house.

3. *If the subject of church comes up.* If at any time the subject of church comes up, use it as a stepping stone to talk about Jesus rather than a detour to get you off of the main issue. For instance, when you mention that you are from church, if they say, "Well, we're Lutherans," say, "That's wonderful" and proceed right on with your conversation

You can be a Soul Winner — Here's How!

of getting into the main issue of Jesus Christ and His way of salvation.

4. *Best not to go in now.* If they give the slightest indication that they would rather you didn't come in now (because of sickness, company, in the middle of the meal, husband sleeping, getting ready to go away, etc.), do not be offended or disappointed. Simply (a) make an appointment for another time, (b) leave some gospel literature, and (c) graciously depart. Proceed something like this:

    "When would be a good time that we could stop by again and visit you?"

    If they do not suggest a definite time, you might make some suggestions. Be sure to nail down, if at all possible, a definite day and time in the near future when you can return. Then leave literature and depart.

    "Here's some literature we'd like to leave with you to read when you get a chance. I think you'll find it very worthwhile. (Pause.) We've certainly enjoyed meeting you, Mrs. Brown. We'll look forward to seeing you at (time) on (day) of next week. Hope you all have a good week. Good-bye for now."

    (Note: Do not use the word *tract.* The average person today is quite unfamiliar with this word. Use *literature, pamphlet, leaflet,* or *brochure* instead.)

5. *If no one is at home.* If no one is at home, leave a Christian leaflet in the door so that something is done to get the gospel into every home. If they want further spiritual help, the church stamp on the back of the leaflet will give them a place to inquire further. Or you may choose to return to the home at a later time.

LEARN A HOME VISITATION PROCEDURE

IV. ENTERING THE LIVING ROOM

A. Introductions

As you enter the living room, greet each person and make sure that all introductions are properly and adequately made. The people in whose home you are calling should take the initiative to make sure that everyone is introduced to everyone. But often they don't, so you will have to.

B. Get the TV off

If you don't get the television set turned off, you won't get into spiritual things, you won't even get acquainted. The best way to do it is to get it turned off before you ever sit down. Simply ask:

"Are you folks watching the television? If you are, we can come back some other time."

Generally they will say that they are not watching anything important and will turn it off. If they do not, proceed with,

"Could it be turned off so we can visit together for a few minutes?"

Occasionally they will indicate that they are watching something important and will ask you to come back. In this case, make an appointment. Then go on and make good use of your evening somewhere else.

Do not sit down or make it seem that you are going to stay until the TV is turned off. The only exception to this is when young children are deeply engrossed in the program. Turning it off at that point might cause more confusion than help. In such cases ask if it can be turned down. In this situation you also may want to suggest that you go somewhere else to talk such as the family room or patio or around the dining room table.

C. Arrange the seating

It is important that the soul winner be seated as near as possible to the unsaved family. The silent worker can greatly help at this point by tactfully and graciously making his way to the single, lonely chair on the other side of the room. This

81

You can be a Soul Winner—Here's How!

leaves the other seats that are nearer to each other for the soul winner and the family.

V. SETTING THE STAGE FOR SOUL WINNING

A. Get acquainted

Take about 15 minutes to relax the family, get acquainted, and talk about things of general interest. Compliment something in the room. Be relaxed, natural, friendly, and gracious yourself. Get acquainted with them and let them get acquainted with you. Discuss the weather and the news (but don't get side-tracked on politics, etc.). Talk about each other's homes, children, work.

Both the soul winner and the silent partner should take part in this time of general conversation. The soul winner should guide, but not monopolize, the conversation by graciously and tactfully injecting questions. Do not discuss politics and other controversial subjects.

Do not discuss church membership. Talking about *church* is one of the devil's easiest detours to keep us from talking about Jesus Christ. We'll go into a home and talk to them about the church building, the pastor, the services, the meetings coming up, the youth program, etc., etc. We talk to them about everything, except Jesus. And the devil will let us do it. He doesn't care how much we talk about the other things as long as we don't talk about Christ. So, don't get on the subject of church. The only exceptions are if it is a new family in the community and they want to know about your church, or if they have attended occasionally and have some questions. Answer their questions, but don't get detoured. Get back to the main issue—Christ.

Do not let the conversation drift on to one topic of special interest to them. If this happens, you may find it hard to get off that topic. The only sure way to change the topic is to ask a question about another subject. For example, if the conversation drifts to fishing, the husband's favorite sport, you will probably have to change it by saying,

"And what ages are your children, Mr. (name)?"

82

LEARN A HOME VISITATION PROCEDURE

Do not let the conversation last too long—usually 15 minutes is long enough.

B. Silent worker begins to baby-sit and pray

As the soul winner and silent partner have the time of general conversation with the family, the silent worker should try to gain the children's interest and begin to baby-sit with them. Here's a place to be informal—get on the floor with them or do whatever else is necessary to gain and keep their interest!

I know a fellow in Michigan who had puppets, candy, etc., in his pockets. I know of at least one home where a baby needed changing and he changed the baby. It needed food and he got the bottle out of the refrigerator, warmed it up, and fed the baby! I remember one time in Oklahoma where a young couple didn't have any children, but they had a dog. That dog was right up in the middle of everything. So my silent partner very wisely took the dog, went to the dining room and got down on the floor and played for 45 minutes with the dog so that I could talk with the young couple about the Lord. As you start to baby-sit, also pray that the soul winner will know when to make the transition.

C. Make the transition

After the proper time for conversation, the soul winner should begin the transition (see Chapter 3). At this point the silent worker becomes silent. From the first transition question through the initial follow-up, the silent worker should baby-sit, pray silently, and let the soul winner do all of the talking with the family. The only exception is if he is asked a personal question, in which case he will answer it, and then let the conversation control immediately return to the soul winner. Even if the soul winner forgets what to say next, remain silent, pray, and wait for the soul winner to ask you (the silent partner) to participate.

If you are visiting for the first time in a new home, and you sense a very definite reluctance to discuss spiritual things with you as you start through the transition, simply (1) leave

83

You can be a Soul Winner — Here's How!

some gospel literature, (2) ask if you could offer a word of prayer, (3) thank them for their time, and (4) graciously depart. Then pray daily for them, return when the Lord tells you to, and start through the transition again. Keep praying (see Chapter 7), keep loving (see Chapter 8), and don't give up. Remember, God is at work.

D. Rearrange the seating

At the end of the last transition question, after the family has consented to look at the Scripture verses, the silent worker may have an additional duty. If he is sitting closer to the family than the soul winner, he can greatly improve the situation by offering his chair to the soul winner.

E. Drink of water

If you know that you are going to a home where the wife is saved and the man is not, it's best to make arrangements ahead of time so that the wife won't be there when you come. And it would be best for two men to go. The reason for this is that an unsaved man many times will be least likely to open up in front of his wife. If you get in a home and there discover that the man is unsaved and the wife is a Christian, you will need to get the wife out of the room. The best way I know how to do this is to ask the wife for a glass of water. When she goes out to the kitchen, follow her and explain to her that you have come to talk with her husband about the Lord and that it would be better if she could find some sewing or something to do in another room. She will understand and be very anxious to cooperate. Then go back into the living room and proceed with the gentleman.

LEARN A HOME VISITATION PROCEDURE

Questions to Answer

1. What are some of the situations of home evangelism recorded in the New Testament?
2. What are the steps in your visitation procedure from the beginning through the place where you are invited into a home?
3. What are the steps from the point where you are inside their front door through to the point where you depart from their home?

Questions for Meditation and Application

1. If you have done soul-winning work in homes before, how can you improve your work based on suggestions given in this chapter?
2. Is the evangelism approach of your church fulfilling the Great Commission in your city? What strategy does your church have to get the gospel to every person in your immediate community? What changes need to be made?
3. Can the evangelism work in your church be improved with a visitation evangelism thrust such as is suggested in this chapter? How can such an effort be incorporated into the existing program? What can you do to get something started?

Assignment

1. Learn this home visitation procedure.
2. Begin to pray for a God-given strategy whereby the gospel can be taken to every person in the immediate community of your church, to every person in the city.

You can be a Soul Winner—Here's How!

Chapter 5

Obtain Soul-winning Equipment

Your last preparation step in becoming an effective, Spirit-filled soul winner is to obtain adequate soul-winning equipment. This is very important. Any job is best done only with proper equipment.

I. A MARKED NEW TESTAMENT

A. Obtain a Testament.

You should obtain a neat, good quality New Testament with large, legible printing. It should be as large as possible, yet small enough to fit in a woman's purse or a man's shirt or coat pocket. Do not use one which is already marked up.

B. Mark your Testament.

Box in, as outlined below, the six Scripture passages used in the soul-winning method by using a ballpoint pen and a straight edge. Notice that in some cases not all of the verse is included in the box. Be extremely careful and NEAT as you do this work. The prospect's opinion of you and your Lord may be based on the neatness of your Testament.

1. Rom. 3:23

> 23 For all have sinned, and come short of the glory of God:

2. Rom. 6:23

> 23 For the wages of sin is death; but the gift of God is eternal life through Jesus Christ our Lord.

3. Acts 3:19

> 19 Repent ye therefore, and be converted, that your sins may be blotted out, when the times of refreshing shall come from the presence of the Lord;

4. Jn. 1:12

> 12 But as many as received him, to them gave he power to become the sons of God even to them that believe on his name:

You can be a Soul Winner — Here's How!

5. Rev. 3:20

> 20 Behold, I stand at the door, and knock: if any one hears My voice and opens the door, I will come in to him, and will dine with him, and he with Me.

6. 1 Jn. 5:11-12

> 11 And this is the record, that God has given to us eternal life, and this life is in his Son.
> 12 He that has the Son has life; and he that has not the Son of God has not life.

C. Tab your Testament

In addition to marking your Testament you will want to tab it in order to quickly turn from one verse to the next. Use 3/8 or 1/2-inch scotch tape. Cut six pieces 1/2- to 5/8-inches long. Fold the first piece around the edge of the page at the top on the right side of the page where Rom. 3:23 appears. Then place a tab farther down the edge of the right side where the second verse appears. Do the same for each verse as shown below. If you are left handed, you may want to put the tape on the left hand side of the page.

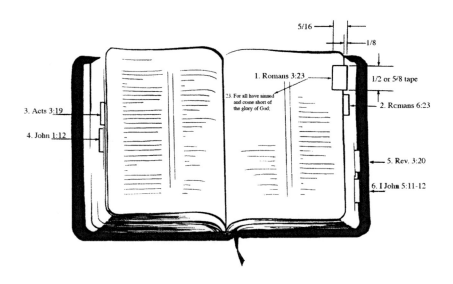

88

OBTAIN SOUL-WINNING EQUIPMENT

II. OTHER EQUIPMENT

A. Witnessing booklets

Order a supply of witnessing booklets.

B. Gospel leaflets

Acquire gospel leaflets to carry with you at all times for use as outlined throughout this book.

C. Stamp your literature

It is suggested that the church name, other Christian organization name, or your name; address; and phone number be stamped or printed on the back of each of these leaflets. If you don't already have a stamp, it is suggested that you get one made that would read something like this:

For further information or guidance, contact:

The Community Church
500 North Atlantic Avenue
Chicago, IL 60644
Phone: 213-123-4567

D. Literature holder

Get a holder for your literature that will fit into your pocket or purse so that your literature will not get wrinkled or soiled.

E. Assignment cards

The church should have assignment cards filled out that tell the witnessing teams where to go. Blank cards should be made available to fill out when the teams run into new prospects. Available cards are listed in Appendix C.

F. Flashlight

Have a flashlight to use in referring to material in your car and to use in checking street names and house numbers. For the latter use, it is suggested that you get out of your car and walk up to the home rather than shining it on homes from your car as you drive down the street.

You can be a Soul Winner—Here's How!

G. Map

Have an area map to help you locate prospects' homes.

III. HELPS FOR NEW CHRISTIANS

A. Leaflets

Get a supply of leaflets to leave with new converts.

B. Testaments and Bibles

Have a supply of New Testaments and/or Bibles to leave with new Christians who do not already have such or who want an easier-to-read translation than they already have.

C. Study booklets

Get a supply of study booklets to use in discipling these new Christians.

Question to Answer

1. What equipment do you need for effective soul winning and follow-up?

Question for Meditation and Application

1. What equipment should you carry with you at all times in order to always be prepared?

Assignment

1. Obtain adequate soul-winning equipment.
2. Mark and tab your Testament.

You can be a Soul Winner—Here's How!

Chapter 6

Locate Evangelism Prospects

Jesus came to seek and save the lost (Lk. 19:10). Likewise, you must seek out unsaved people before you can begin to help them spiritually. Your first step, therefore, in beginning to win souls is to locate evangelism prospects. Your two best sources for evangelism prospects are your local church and your daily life.

I. PROSPECTS THROUGH YOUR CHURCH

A. Tabulating evangelism prospects on the fringe of the church

One of the simplest and best ways to locate evangelism prospects is to simply tabulate those prospects that are already on the *fringe* of the church. These are people who already have some contact with your church and in a sense are looking to you for spiritual guidance. In many cases, they are spiritually hungry and should be the first that you consider going to to present the gospel of Jesus Christ.

For each of these prospects for evangelism, regardless of how located, a Prospect Card should be filled out as completely as possible. In Appendix C, you will find a sample of a Prospect Card. Section B explains how to fill out this card.

1. *Visitors.* Every person who visits any meeting of the church even one time should be considered a prospect for evangelism. A Prospect Card should be filled out on that family and put into the Evangelism Prospect File for future assignment to witnessing teams.

2. *Sunday School, etc., Families.* Prospect Cards should be made out on every home represented by a Sunday school child. If the boy or girl comes to Sunday school, a Prospect Card should be made out on that family and a trained team of soul winners should get into the home as soon as possible to talk with the parents about Jesus. A

You can be a Soul Winner — Here's How!

Prospect Card should likewise be made out on the family of every child who attends Daily Vacation Bible School, boys' clubs, girls' clubs, etc. In other words, every home that in any way is in contact with the church should be considered a prospect for evangelism. A card should be made out for that home, and a team should get into the home to witness at the earliest opportunity.

3. *Bus Routes.* A card should be filled out for every home where anyone rides one of the buses provided by a church bus route ministry.

4. *Pastor's contacts.* Most pastors make contact with more new unsaved people through hospital visits, funerals, weddings, etc., than they have time to get back to and personally confront with the Gospel of Jesus Christ in their homes. Therefore, a Prospect Card should be made out for each of these homes and put into the Evangelism Prospect File for teams to visit.

5. *New families in the community.* Many communities have a Welcome Wagon or Newcomers List that the church can subscribe to for a minimum fee. With this service, the name and address of every new family moving into the community will be forwarded to the church office. Each of these names and addresses should then be put on a Prospect Card and the card put into the card file for future assignment to witnessing teams. Sometimes this service is also available through one of the utility companies.

6. *Individual Contacts.* Each person in the church should be encouraged to fill out Prospect Cards on any individuals or families that they personally know are in need of Jesus. This might include a wide variety of people (their neighbors, people they work with, etc.) whom they feel a witnessing team should visit to talk about Jesus Christ and His wonderful way of salvation.

In conclusion, a Prospect Card should be made out on every individual or family which is in any way considered a prospect for evangelism. These should all be arranged in a card file. See Section III of this chapter for how to set up such

LOCATE EVANGELISM PROSPECTS

a file. Then these many homes should be assigned to witnessing teams to be visited during the weekly visitation evangelism work.

B. Filling out the evangelism prospect card

The Evangelism Prospect Card should be filled out initially as completely as possible. Additional information should be added to it whenever such information becomes available, i.e., as you get to know them better. But do not fill out the card in their presence.

The Prospect Card should be filled out as follows:

1. Front side

   Age of parents: Circle the appropriate age (young, middle-aged, older) category.

   House number: Put the house number—also any appropriate apartment number or letter.

   Street name: Give the appropriate street name—also give the name of the community if there is any chance of confusion with another near-by community.

   Best time to call: Circle the best time to call category or categories.

   Last name: Give the last name if it is the same for everyone in the home. If it is not the same for everyone in the home, give the name of the parents of the home; also give the full name (first and last) in First Name section for each person.

   Occupation: Give the occupations of the parents.

   Phone: Give the home phone number.

   Responsible worker: Fill in only if someone feels a burden to take the family as *his* responsibility to reach for the Lord. In this case, the card will be given out only to him.

   First name and age: List the first name and age of each person in the home.

You can be a Soul Winner—Here's How!

Church and Sunday School attendance: List where each person attends church and Sunday school and whether they attend regularly (R) or occasionally (O).

Remarks: Put any additional information that might be helpful to those who may be visiting in the home in the future. Examples might be: His father was a Baptist preacher. They watch Billy Graham on television. He is very hard. Their teenage son attends Young Life meetings.

Census taker and date: Put the name of the person who initially fills out the card and the date that it is filled out.

2. Back side

Each time a team goes to visit in a home, an accurate, detailed report should be given including date, workers' names, and what took place during the visit, i.e., progress in discussing spiritual things, literature left, suggestions as to when to return, etc. The report should be as specific as possible.

C. Defining an area for total evangelization

Another excellent way to locate evangelism prospects and to actually be involved in evangelism work at the same time is by door-to-door witnessing. The first step in getting involved in door-to-door witnessing is to define an area in your community, often the area in the vicinity of the church building, to which you are going. For even the very smallest church, this area should initially contain 10 to 20 blocks and many churches should consider an area containing 25-50 blocks. It is suggested that you get a good-sized map of the city and take a felt pen and actually mark on the map the area to which, as a church, you are going to take the gospel.

Then you will want to fill out Witnessing Assignment Sheets. See Appendix D for a sample of this sheet. One sheet should be filled out for each block in your area that you have defined in your city. To fill out the Assignment Sheet, simply put the four street names around the block, which will indicate to the team exactly which block they are going to cover. If you live

96

LOCATE EVANGELISM PROSPECTS

in a new suburban area where the streets are not laid off in straight lines or are in the country where, likewise, the roads are not straight, it is suggested that you cross off the block and in the blank area provided to the left of it draw the street or area a given team should cover.

The names of the team members who cover this particular area and the date that they do the work will be filled in at the top by them after they receive the assignment sheet. Likewise, the report of the area they covered will be described by them after they are through with their work by filling out the report section on the bottom of the sheet. The report should include the number of the house where they terminated their work so that the block can be finished later. Areas that are not completely covered should later be given to the same team or another team to complete.

In using the W.A.S., one can start at any corner of the assigned block and go in either direction as long as the report clearly indicates how much of the block has been covered and how much remains to be covered in the future.

Having defined an area for total evangelization and having prepared the Witnessing Assignment Sheet for each block in the area, you are now ready to send teams out to cover the area block-by-block in any one or more of the types of door-to-door witnessing described in sections D–H.

D. Giving away free Christian literature

One of the best approaches to door-to-door witnessing is to give away free Christian literature.

1. *Order literature.* To prepare for this, you will want to order a supply of gospel literature that can be used in this kind of work.

2. *Stamp literature.* Stamp the literature with your organizational stamp as explained in Chapter 5.

3. *Put into packets.* The stamped leaflets should be put in packs of 25 each with a rubber band around each pack. This is based on the assumption that the average city block contains 25 or less homes.

You can be a Soul Winner—Here's How!

4. *Blank prospects cards.* Blank Prospect Cards should also be put into packets. A pack of 15 cards per team should be sufficient.

5. *Witnessing Assignment Sheet.* Witnessing Assignment Sheets should be filled out in preparation for the door-to-door work. See Section C of this chapter.

6. *Going door-to-door.* After a time of training and prayer, each team should be given a Witnessing Assignment Sheet telling them which block to cover, a packet of Christian literature, and a packet of blank Prospect Cards.

7. *At the door.* The approach at the door should include the greeting and introduction as outlined in Chapter 4. Then proceed with giving the purpose of your visit.

   "Hello. We're from the church down on the corner. And we're out in the neighborhood this afternoon leaving some Christian literature with our neighbors. We'd like to leave this with you to read when you have time if we may."

   The team spokesman would hand the leaflet to the person at this point. Then proceed with, **"This isn't about the church. (Pause) You can tell by the title that it's about how we can come to know God. And what He can mean in our lives. I don't know if you folks have thought much about this kind of thing or not?"** You see that now you are in the transition (see Chapter 3). So you can use a leaflet or booklet, mention the title, tell them that it isn't about the church but it's about Jesus. And then start through the transition.

   As you move on through the transition, the interview will conclude with a) an invitation to come in because they would like to see what the Bible has to say about this; b) a definite appointment to come back some time in the future to discuss spiritual things; or c) a termination of the conversation because the family is not interested in discussing with you further Jesus Christ and His way of salvation.

LOCATE EVANGELISM PROSPECTS

Be sure to try to leave literature with every home. Also, leave literature in the door where no one is at home. In this way, if you never get back, you have done something to get the gospel into every home. And with the church stamp on the literature, they will know of at least one place where they can get further help if they want it.

8. *Situations that may develop.* Don't forget to be ready for situations that may develop (if a woman or child answers the door, if the subject of *church* comes up, etc.) as outlined in Chapter 4.

9. *Filling out the Prospect Card.* Do not fill out the card in front of the people. Fill it out when you get back out on the sidewalk, between this home and the next one, or between apartments in an apartment building.

   Do not fill out a card on every home. Only fill out a Prospect Card on the homes where someone should definitely return. Remember, it doesn't have anything to do with church membership or church attendance. They may go to church, they may not go to church. It doesn't matter. That isn't the issue. The issue is whether they know the Lord or not. And if they don't, whether or not they are open to hear about Him. Fill out a card on the homes a) where you were invited in; b) where you made an appointment to come back; or c) where you sense that the family is open to learn more about Jesus and His wonderful way of salvation. In this way, you have a card on each family that is a prospect for evangelism.

10. *Turn the card in.* These cards should be turned in to the Minister of Evangelism to be placed in the file (see Section III) for future assignment to witnessing teams.

E. Community Religious Survey

Another approach that can be used in door-to-door witnessing is the Community Religious Survey. See Appendix E for a sample of a survey sheet, or you may want to develop your own survey sheet.

You can be a Soul Winner—Here's How!

With this approach, each team should be given a Witnessing Assignment Sheet telling them what area to cover, a clipboard containing 25 survey forms, and a packet of Christian leaflets to leave at the door at the conclusion of the survey.

The approach at the door is included right on the survey. The team will go as far in the survey with the family as they are open to go. The survey will, in many cases, result in an invitation to go in to present the way of salvation to the family. A second possibility will be the making of a definite appointment to come back and talk further with the family at a later time. Leave literature for them to read in the meantime. If neither of these open up, a third alternative would be to simply leave a piece of literature with them to read.

After leaving the home, between that home and the next one, the interviewers will want to complete the bottom portion of the survey sheet. Evangelism Prospect Cards should then be completed as outlined in Section D-9.

F. Selling Christian Books

Another approach that can be used in door-to-door witnessing is to sell good Christian literature from house to house.

You will want to order a supply of these books and stamp the church stamp on the inside of the back cover or some other appropriate place. Each team would fill a briefcase with a quantity of several items that are going to be offered for sale, be given a Witnessing Assignment Sheet indicating what block to cover, and be given a packet of Christian leaflets and a packet of Prospect Cards.

The approach at the door would be similar to that in the preceding sections—greeting, telling where you are from, and explaining your purpose. Have samples of a few books in your hand to show the people as you introduce yourselves.

"Good afternoon, we are from the (name) Church at (address). We are in the neighborhood this afternoon making available to our neighbors some good, inexpensive Christian books for them to purchase and have in their

LOCATE EVANGELISM PROSPECTS

homes in these days of turmoil that we find ourselves living in. Would you care to see what we have available?"

One of the Christian leaflets should be left at every home—those who buy, those who don't buy, and those who aren't home.

A Prospect Card should be made out between that home and the next one for every home that seems open to the gospel. You will want to indicate in the remarks section of the Prospect Card exactly which items they purchased.

Then in about a month, a witnessing team can go back to the home to see if they have had a chance to read the materials, to get acquainted with them, and to discuss spiritual things further with them (as outlined in Chapter 3).

G. The results of a census

Taking a census of the thousands of homes that surround your church is another way to locate evangelism prospects.

Not just any census, however, will do. The usual census, which reveals little more than people's church preference, is inadequate. You must use a census system which finds out where each person in your census area attends church and how often he attends.

1. *Prepare Materials.* Get a supply of gospel literature ordered, stamped (see Chapter 5), and put into packets, 25 per pack. Put the Prospect Cards into packets of 25. Prepare Witnessing Assignment Sheets (see Section C).

2. *Training.* Have a time of training and prayer. Each team should be given a Witness Assignment Sheet, telling them what block(s) to cover, a packet of Cards, and a packet of gospel literature.

3. *Going Door-to-Door.* Stop at each house. Greet them. Tell them where you are from. Tell them you are taking a census and ask for their cooperation.

   "Good afternoon, Sir. We are from the First Baptist Church. We are taking a Religious Census. May we ask you where you attend church?" (Pause for answer.)

101

You can be a Soul Winner — Here's How!

"And how often?" (Pause for answer.) **"Thank you, Sir. May we leave this little booklet with you to read when you have time?"** (Hand it to them.) **"Thank you so much for your cooperation."**

4. *Using the information.* Turn the completed cards in to the Minister of Evangelism to be placed in the file (see Section III) for future assignment to witnessing teams.

Until you make further contact with the censused homes and begin to *feel them out* spiritually you can assume that every family is a potential evangelism prospect except those who regularly attend an evangelical church.

H. Invitation to a meeting

Another approach that can be used in door-to-door witnessing is to prepare printed invitations to a special meeting that is going to be conducted at the church. This may be an evangelistic crusade or revival meeting, or some other type of meeting such as a youth fellowship, men's breakfast, a special series dealing with family problems, etc. It may also be a meeting that is going to be conducted in someone's home in the neighborhood such as an informal time of discussion about spiritual things, a neighborhood Bible study, a ladies' coffee cup Bible study meeting, etc.

The approach at the door would include 1) the greeting; 2) telling what church (in the case of a church-centered meeting) or neighborhood (in the case of a home-centered meeting) you are from; 3) explaining the purpose of being there; 4) giving them a leaflet and telling them a little about the meeting; and 5) then at the conclusion of each door contact also leave with the family some gospel literature that tells about Jesus Christ and His way of salvation.

A discussion may develop at either the presentation of the invitation to the meeting or at the presentation of the gospel literature, and in either case the worker should try to direct the conversation toward Jesus Christ. Such an encounter at the door may lead to 1) an invitation to come in to discuss spiritual things in more depth; 2) an appointment to come back for the same; or 3) a feeling on the worker's part that

102

LOCATE EVANGELISM PROSPECTS

someone should return. In any of these cases, a Prospect Card should be made out. These should be turned in to the Minister of Evangelism for future assignment to witnessing teams.

I. Telephone survey

Another approach that can be used in door-to-door witnessing (without going to the door) is the telephone survey using the Community Religious Survey modified for telephone use (see Appendix F for a sample).

With this approach, each volunteer caller is given a number of calls to make either alphabetically from an alphabetical directory or numerically from a street directory. He should also be given a number of Survey Sheets.

The approach and conversation to be used are included right on the Survey Sheet. Let the phone ring five times before hanging up. The caller should go as far in the survey as the person is willing to go. If a child answers, the caller should ask to speak with one of the parents. Be open to the possibility of leading them to the Lord right over the phone.

Evangelism Prospect Cards should then be completed for all homes where an appointment has been made.

A good gospel leaflet should be mailed to all who were not open to visit but who did give permission for something to be sent.

If they are a Christian, spend a few minutes in fellowship with them—encourage them in the things of the Lord.

J. Through your Personal Evangelism Work

The church needs to have a day a week for Personal Evangelism as outlined in Chapter 9. As you are involved in going out to homes of prospects, you will meet people along the way that you did not intend to meet, such as homes where prospects have moved away. These are now prospects, too. Make out a Prospect Card on them when you get back in your car.

You can be a Soul Winner — Here's How!

II. PROSPECTS THROUGH YOUR DAILY LIVING

Another excellent way, and in many ways the best, to find prospects is through your daily living. You are in touch with the world in a very wonderful way, in fact, in a way which probably far surpasses that of your pastor.

Besides this, your responsibility for finding prospects is one you have received from the Lord (Lk. 19:10). He has given you the task of soul winning and part of this task is to find prospects. Become soul conscious. Begin to see every person you see, know, and meet as one who needs the Lord.

A. Using Christian leaflets

Begin at once to carry gospel tracts with you. They should be neat, unwrinkled, clean, legible, and attractive and should clearly and simply explain the way of salvation or be the story of someone's conversion. Men can carry them in a folder in the inside pocket of their suit coat or their shirt pocket and women can carry them in a folder in their purse.

Give them out freely throughout the course of the day to people you know and to strangers. Leave one with the mailman, the gas station attendant, the cleaners, the grocer, your fellow employee, your teacher, the beauty parlor attendant, the paper boy—and on the list could go. These are people who need the Lord.

As you pay your bills or have other contact with these people, graciously, tactfully, and wisely hand them a leaflet and say something like this,

"We certainly have enjoyed your wonderful service these months. I'd like to leave this leaflet with you which tells about the Lord Jesus and how He can transform a person's life."

Your comments will be varied each time, but be sure to (1) compliment the person; (2) make a comment to let them know how wonderful and important the message is; and (3) give a word of personal testimony. Remember to be gracious, tactful, wise and loving—you are an ambassador for Jesus Christ (2 Cor. 5:20).

104

LOCATE EVANGELISM PROSPECTS

Some of the people you give literature to you'll never see again. But the seed has been sown which the Holy Spirit will water, and someone else will harvest (Jn. 4:37). Many of these people you will see again. Ask them what they thought of the leaflet the next time you see them. As you have further contact with them, continue to cultivate their friendship and to briefly discuss spiritual things with them. Ask the Lord for an opportunity to make an appointment.

Your appointment conversation might go something like this,

"It's sure good to see you again, (name). It's wonderful to know that you're thinking about spiritual things. I would love to have the privilege of getting together with you sometime and showing you from the Bible some more about this." (Pause) **"Would you be interested in this?"**

Don't get discouraged if he doesn't suggest a time right away. Remember he needs the Lord, and you're probably closer to winning him than anyone else has ever been. Hold steady, keep praying, keep cultivating, and keep waiting for your chance. The day will come when you'll see him saved.

B. Making opportunities

In addition to prospects which you can find through the use of Christian literature, there are others that the Holy Spirit will lead you to as you go about your daily living. Yield yourself to the Holy Spirit for His use and ask Him to give you open doors. Then expect doors to open!

You will find many opportunities for witnessing. And some of these you can talk to about the Lord in a more thorough way later by making an appointment with them. Consider every contact with people as a possible soul-winning contact. As you follow the Lord's leading, start through the transition (Chapter 3) with many of these contacts. Reword the last transition question as follows:

"Would you be interested in seeing what the Bible has to say about this? Maybe we could get together sometime when we both have a little more time." (Pause) **"When would be a good time?"**

You can be a Soul Winner—Here's How!

C. Going on-line

You can find spiritually hungry people by going to chat rooms on-line. Bring up the subject of spiritual things, find hungry souls, begin to chat with them, and eventually lead them to Christ. We have a friend that has become quite effective at this.

III. SETTING UP A FILE OF EVANGELISM PROSPECTS

The Prospect Card in Appendix C should be enlarged and reproduced in a 5" x 8" size. A file box for them can be purchased at most office supply stores in a variety of price ranges. You will also want to get a supply of index cards to separate the prospect cards within the file.

There are various ways that the Prospects Cards can be grouped within the file box. Some possibilities include arranging them alphabetically by street name, alphabetically by the family's last name, and geographically according to sections of the city.

The most common way is to divide the prospects into definite geographic areas, such as those who live north of the church, those who live east of the church, etc. You would make out a divider card for each of these sections. The families in that section would then be filed alphabetically by last name behind that particular divider card.

You may also want to have several special sections including

- Next Week—where cards can be filed where definite appointments have been made or where teams should definitely try to get to next week.

- In Two Weeks—for the same purpose as above, except for two weeks from today.

- For the Pastor—where cards on families that need the Pastor's personal visit can be placed.

- Follow-Up—where cards of new converts can be filed.

It is very important to have a practical, systematic, workable file that is set up, kept up to date, and made an integral part of your evangelism work. Systems may vary from church to church, but it is important to have a system that works—and then work it!

LOCATE EVANGELISM PROSPECTS

Questions to Answer

1. What must you do before you can begin to help people to the Savior? (Lk. 19:10)?
2. In what ways can you get evangelism prospects through your church?
3. How can you locate evangelism prospects through your daily living?

Questions for Meditation and Application

1. What are you doing to get in contact with unsaved people? In what ways can you improve?
2. How can you begin to distribute Christian literature as part of your daily life?
3. Is the Holy Spirit using you at your place of employment? Have you yet yielded to Him? How can you more effectively be God's witness on the job?

You can be a Soul Winner—Here's How!

Chapter 7

Pray for Your Prospects

Your next step in beginning to bring people to Jesus Christ is to begin to pray for them.

I. THE IMPORTANCE OF INTERCESSION

It has been said that prayer is the greatest force in the universe. This is true! Prayer releases the power of God! "Call unto me, and I will answer thee, and show thee great and mighty things, which thou knowest not" (Jer. 33:3). In effect, God has limited Himself to the prayers of His people.

Prayer takes different forms.

- There is *adoration*—worshiping God (Ex. 15:2; Ps. 149:1; Jn. 4:23)

- There is *confessing* our sins to God (2 Sam. 24:10; Neh. 1:6; 1 Jn. 1:9)

- There is *thanksgiving*—thanking Him for who He is, for what He is doing (1 Ki. 8:56; Ps. 107:1; Eph. 5:20)

- There is *intercession*—praying for others—people, groups, nations, etc. (Ex. 32:11-14; Ezek. 22:30; 1 Tim. 2:1)

- There is *supplication*—praying for our own needs (1 Ki. 18:36; Ps. 4:1; 1 Th. 3:10)

History is the story of intercessory people who cared—**Moses** (Ex. 32:31-32; Num. 12:11-13, 14:13-19; Dt. 9:25-29; Ps. 106:23); **Samuel** (1 Sam. 7:5-10); **David** (1 Chr. 21:14-17); **Jesus Christ** (Isa. 53:12; Lk. 23:34; Jn. 14:16, 17:9; Heb. 7:25); and **Paul** (Rom. 1:9; Eph. 1:16, 3:14; Phil. 1:4; Col 1:3; 1 Th. 1:2). These are just a few examples. Likewise God is looking for people in our day who will give themselves to intercession. As you pray Spirit-led prayers, you can create with God. By the Holy Spirit's direction you can think God's thoughts, pray God's prayers, feel God's feelings, speak God's words, and do God's work.

You can be a Soul Winner—Here's How!

II. HOW TO INTERCEDE

A. The following are principles of intercession that will assist you as you move into a ministry of intercession.

1. Get to *know* the *God* to whom you pray. Study passages that tell us of His character—His love, His mercy, His faithfulness, His justice, etc. Begin by studying Ps. 139, 145, Neh. 9, Dan. 10, Ezek. 1, and Rev. 1. Ask God to give you a *revelation* of Himself.

2. Our *only right* to come to God is on the basis of the *atonement* of Jesus Christ. This is why we pray in *His name* (Heb.10: 19-20; Jn. 14:13, 15:16, 16:24, 16:26).

3. You must pray with the *right motive*. Your only desire must be to glorify God. Whose glory and purposes are you praying about—yours or God's? (Mt. 6:9, 6:33; Jn. 17:4; Jas. 4:3).

4. You must pray *according to God's will*. Coupling 1 Jn. 5:14 with 2 Pet. 3:9 gives grounds for authoritatively praying for the salvation of others throughout the world.

5. Pray in *faith*. God will do what you believe Him for (Mt. 21:21-22; Mk. 11:22-24; Jas. 1:6-7; Heb. 11:6; Rom. 14:23).

6. Use God's Word to *reason* with Him as you pray. Pray with an open Bible. Base your praying upon His Word, His promises, His power, and His faithfulness (Isa. 41:21; Rom. 4:20-21).

B. The following are steps to follow as you begin to enter a time of intercession. (These have been adapted with permission from teaching by Joy Dawson of Youth With A Mission.)

1. Make sure you are *without offense* toward God and toward men. All channels must be open—vertically (to God) and horizontally (to man) to pray effectively (Ps. 66:18; Acts 24:16; Ps. 139: 23-24; 2 Chr. 7:14).

PRAY FOR YOUR PROSPECTS

2. Acknowledge that you cannot pray without the direction and energy of the *Holy Spirit*. Ask God to fill you afresh with His Spirit (Rom. 8:26-27; Eph. 5:18).

3. Ask for the *fear of God* so that you will pray all that, and only that, which He leads you to pray (Prov. 29:25; Acts 5:29).

4. Pray with *authority* to defeat the enemy of God, Satan. Come against him in the mighty name of Jesus (Eph. 6:12; Mt. 12:29; 1 Pet. 5:8-9; Jas. 4:7).

5. *Die to your own imaginations*, desires, and burdens—those things that you are thinking about and that you want to pray—so that God can lead you to pray the things that *He wants* you to pray (Prov. 3:5-6, 28:26; Isa. 55:8; 2 Cor. 10:5).

6. Wait in silent *expectancy*. Then, in obedience and faith, pray out what God prompts you to pray. Pray as you feel led or *prompted* to pray. Let the Holy Spirit be your prayer teacher/leader (Jn. 10:3-4, 27; Eph. 6:18; Jude 20).

For added power, find a prayer partner or form a prayer group. Such a group should be kept small so that all can participate. Ask God to knit you together (Mt. 18:18-20). Meet on a daily, weekly, or monthly basis. Have a map handy to refer to as God leads you to pray for various nations. Keep a diary of what God leads you to pray so that you can refer back to it as things you are led to pray come to pass.

As you pray for unsaved friends, pray that God will open their hearts (Acts 16:14), show them their sinful condition (Jn. 16:8), show them their need for Christ (Jn. 15:26), and that they will soon respond (2 Pet. 3:9). As you pray for yourself and your fellow Christians, pray for a vision and true compassion to evangelize (Prov. 29:18), for a burden for the lost (Isa. 66:8), and for laborers to be sent into the harvest (Mt. 9:37-38). Pray for the evangelization of the world in this generation.

Complement your daily morning times of prayer and your prayer group times with some periodic extended seasons of prayer. Be instrumental in starting an all-night prayer meeting in your home or church the first Friday of every month to pray with

You can be a Soul Winner — Here's How!

other such groups around the world for (1) a world-wide awakening and outpouring of the Holy Spirit and (2) an evangelistic outreach which will get the gospel to every person in the world in this generation. Also remember to spend extra time in prayer during the daytime on the days in which you will be doing soul winning in the evening (Chapter 9).

Don't be concerned about praying long prayers or fancy prayers. Just talk to God! He doesn't want fanciness—He does want *honesty*. Tell Him your every sin, failure, problem, worry, fear, need, and desire. Remember, He loves you.

III. THE PLACE OF FASTING

The practice of fasting is an integral part of biblical prayer. This was the practice of our Lord (Mt. 4:1-2, 17: 14-21; Lk. 4:1-2), of the early Church (Acts 13:2-3, 14:23), and of God's great servants throughout history—Moses (Ex. 34:28), David (Ps. 35:13, 69:10; 2 Sam. 3:35, 12:16), Elijah (1 Ki. 19:8), Daniel (Dan. 10:2-3), Ezra (Ezra 10:1-8), and Paul (Acts 9:9; 2 Cor. 6:5, 11:27).

A. The purposes for fasting are:

1. To permit extra time for seasons of prayer (Ps. 35:13; 2 Sam. 12:16; Joel 1:13-15; 1 Cor. 7:5).
2. To humble the soul (Ps. 35:13, 69:10; Isa. 58:5).
3. For spiritual power (Mt. 17:14-21).
4. To permit extended times of waiting upon God (Ex. 34:28; Jud. 20:26; 1 Ki. 19:8). It is to be done particularly at times of crises and decision making (Ps. 35:13, 69:10; Joel 1:13-15, 2:12; Jud. 20:26; 2 Sam. 12:16; Ezra 10:1-8; Dan. 10:2-3; Mt. 4:1-2; Lk. 4:1-2; Acts 13:2-3).

B. The Bible records periods of fasting consisting of:

1. All day (Jud. 20:26; 1 Sam. 7:6; 2 Sam. 3:35).
2, All night (Dan. 6:18).
3. Three days (Acts 9:9).
4. Seven days (1 Sam. 31:13, 1 Chr. 10:12).
5. Three weeks (Dan. 10:2-3).

PRAY FOR YOUR PROSPECTS

6. Forty days and nights (Ex. 34:28; 1 Ki. 19:8; Mt. 4:1-2; Lk. 4:1-2)

Your times of fasting and prayer should be done with honest heart searching (Isa. 58:1-7; Jer. 14:10-12; Zech. 7:4-7), with weeping (Ps. 69:10; Joel 2:12; Jud. 20:26; 2 Sam. 1:12; Ezra 10:1-8), and in true repentance (Joel 1:13-15, 2:12; 1 Sam. 7:6; 1 Ki. 21:27; Ezra 10:1-8; Neh. 9:1-3). It may be done privately (Mt. 6:6-18; Acts 10:30; Dan. 10:2-3) or with others of like heart (Neh. 9:1-3; 1 Sam. 7:6; Acts 13:2-3).

Begin to develop the habit of fasting and spending much time in prayer and intercession on the day of your evangelism work. Once this one-day-a-week habit is established, you can begin to add to it in order to develop a habit of true biblical prayer and fasting.

You are encouraged to learn all you can about prayer from a host of books and ministries that are available today.

You can be a Soul Winner—Here's How!

Questions to Answer
1. What are the twelve principles of prayer set forth in this chapter?
2. What are some of the principles of fasting as outlined in this chapter?
3. Turn to the appropriate Scripture references given in the first section of this chapter. For what were these men interceding?

Questions for Meditation and Application
1. How can you begin to apply God's promise in Jer. 33:3 to your life?
2. How can you begin to have a greater ministry of intercessory prayer?
3. How must you rearrange your schedule to permit more and regular time for prayer and fasting?

Assignment
1. Begin to spend more time in private prayer.
2. Become part of a prayer group to pray for the needs of the world.
3. Begin to develop the discipline of fasting.

Chapter 8

Cultivate Your Prospects

You are in touch with unsaved people and are praying daily for them. Now you must begin to cultivate a friendship with them and to let them know that you sincerely love them for Christ's sake (2 Cor. 5:14; 1 Th. 3:12).

This means going to them (1 Jn. 4:10). This means getting next to them, associating yourself with them, and in many ways becoming like them, as did our Lord (2 Cor. 8:9; Phil. 2:5-7; Lk. 7:34). This means going out of your way to serve them (1 Cor. 9:19-22, 10:33) and to care for their needs (Lk. 10:33-35).

Go out of your way to be with them. Win their friendship and confidence. Show them that you love them. Overlook all of their bad habits and sinful ways—see them and love them as Jesus did. See them with the Lord's compassionate eyes (Mt. 9:36).

Men, go fishing with them and do other things which they like to do. Take a coffee break with them. Ladies, bake a pie and take it over. See if you can babysit with the children some time. Listen to their interests and problems. Let yourself get involved in their life. Have them over to your home for a meal or an evening (Heb. 13:2; Rom. 12:13).

Each time you see them, silently say to yourself, "God loves that guy." And say silently to them, "God loves you, Joe, and wants to save you."

The author of this book found the Lord Jesus while a college student. The one who was instrumental in bringing him to the Lord used to put him to bed when he came home drunk, shine his shoes before dates, and stop to eat every meal in the dorm dining hall with him. What love and concern!

Do whatever is needful to win their friendship and confidence. Jesus was a *friend of sinners* (Lk. 7:34). Should we be less?

You can be a Soul Winner — Here's How!

Questions to Answer
1. How did Jesus look on the multitudes? (Mt. 9:36)
2. What was the Lord known as? (Lk. 7:34)
3. What does the Bible say is involved in cultivating prospects? (Study passages given in this chapter.)

Questions for Meditation and Application
1. Do you really love unsaved people? Have you ever asked God to use you as an instrument of His love to reach them for Him?
2. What are you doing to meet and get next to people without Christ? Are you a friend of sinners? What do you purpose to do to remedy the situation?
3. How can you begin to win the confidence of your unsaved friends? What do you purpose to do? When and how?

Assignment
1. Begin to get next to your unsaved acquaintances.

Chapter 9

Present Christ to Your Prospects

You are now at one of the most wonderful, thrilling, and important days of your life. Your preparation for soul winning is complete (Chapter 1-5). You have located prospects (Chapter 6). You are praying for them (Chapter 7). You have their confidence (Chapter 8). You now are ready to go to them and tell them about your Savior. As you go, the Lord will bless your efforts, your own Christian life will transform before your very eyes, and many will come to Him.

I. THE IMPORTANCE OF GETTING STARTED

You only become a fisher of men as you fish. There are things you must learn before you start, which is the reason for this book, but you finally only become an effective personal soul winner as you win souls. After progressing this far, you only have one thing left to do—*begin to go*. And the sooner you begin the better. You must put your newly-acquired zeal and knowledge into immediate use or you will lose it. Ask God to open a way that you can make an appointment with someone *this very day*.

II. SETTING ASIDE ONE DAY A WEEK

We only do the things we find time to do. And so it is in soul winning. It's easy to think about bringing men to Christ, and to even plan to get started, but you'll never begin until you set aside a definite time for it.

Set aside one evening a week if you work in the daytime. Evening workers will want to go in the daytime. Ask the Holy Spirit to give you open doors for appointments so that you can be telling people about your wonderful Lord one evening each week. This evening can be in conjunction with your local church Outreach Day or Personal Evangelism Day if it has one. If not, you begin to go one evening a week anyway. Find another Christian and train him to be your silent worker. Your Christian friends and your church will soon be following your example.

You can be a Soul Winner — Here's How!

The Outreach Day is another *absolute necessity* in order to have a soul-winning church and consider total evangelization of the area it serves. It is one day every week set aside for nothing but personal soul winning. It must be considered the *most important day*, except Sunday, in the life of the church and in the lives of the members. Nothing else should interfere. It is on this day that the church begins to contact the thousands of prospects located through many sources.

Everyone who has taken part in the church-wide personal evangelism training should be encouraged to participate. Some will go as soul winners and an equal number as silent workers. There is also a place for those who were not able to take part in the training. They can learn by going as a silent worker and observing the soul winner at work. Also a group needs to stay at the church and pray.

There may be an Evangelism Coordinator to handle much of the administration and coordination of this great work. There may also be a Minister of Evangelism to give leadership to this work. But this does not excuse the Pastor from participating. His *personal participation* is an *absolute necessity*. A church will go no further in soul winning than its leaders.

Prior to your visitation work, the Pastor, Minister of Evangelism, or Personal Evangelism Coordinator should prayerfully look through the Prospect Cards in the file box and pull out those that need to be visited. There may be some homes where an appointment is already made. These, of course, should be visited as per appointment. There will be other homes that are new prospects. These should be visited as soon as possible. There will be others where teams have already called, and these should be re-visited anywhere from once a week to once a month, depending on how the Holy Spirit leads. At this point, it is very important for the Minister of Evangelism to go through the card file very prayerfully, trying to get the mind of the Lord as to exactly which homes should be visited this particular week. The cards for the homes to be visited should be pulled out of the box and put into packets of five cards—all of which are in the same general geographical area so that the teams will not waste time traveling

PRESENT CHRIST TO YOUR PROSPECTS

from one home to the next. The cards should also be grouped according to age as much as possible so that the young couples will be going to young couples, etc. If teams get into homes, generally they will spend the entire evening in one or two homes. But the family of the first home they go to may be away; the people of the second home may have company; and it may be a few homes before the team reaches that place the Lord has for them to be that evening. So, it is important to give each team a pack of five cards to insure that they will find one or two where they can make a profitable visit.

The Prospect Cards should be grouped into packs of five ahead of the preparation meeting whenever possible so that time is not wasted in that meeting trying to regroup them. See to it that good gospel literature is stamped and ready to use ahead of time and also prepare follow-up materials including leaflets for new converts, everyday English translations of the New Testament, and Bible study materials for new Christians.

The workers will assemble at the given hour, often 7 p.m. Seven to seven-thirty will be spent in a time of prayer and preparation. This will include spending time in prayer; teaming up the people, each soul winner having a silent partner to go with him; giving out the assignment packs of Prospect Cards; making available the literature and maps of the city; giving any last minute instructions or words from the scripture; and concluding with a word of prayer before parting.

As the team travels toward the first home, they will talk over their visits and spend time in prayer. Throughout the evening, each team should make a very complete and accurate record of what transpires in each visit on the back of the Prospect Card. Also, any additional information about the family that is missing from the front side of the card, which naturally becomes available by the team getting to know the family better, should be filled in when the team gets back to the car.

The teams should leave the church at about 7:30 and plan to meet back at the church at approximately 9:00 p.m. This gives an hour and a half for good solid visitation and soul-winning work. And, of course, a team who gets involved past 9:00 p.m. should stay

You can be a Soul Winner — Here's How!

and finish what the Lord has for them to do regardless of how late that should be. In most cases, the teams will be able to be back at the church at approximately 9:00 for a time of sharing what took place at the visits, asking questions of the Minister of Evangelism, learning from one another, praying together, rejoicing together, and learning new and wonderful lessons of soul winning from each other's visits.

The cards should be handed back in and filed back into the file box where they will be safely kept until the next time of witnessing, which will probably be on the same evening the following week.

After a family has come to know the Lord and the follow-up work with the new Christians begins, you may continue to use the same Prospect Card keeping a record on the back and filing in the same file box just as prior to their conversion.

III. OPPORTUNITIES THROUGHOUT THE DAY

As you win souls through your church's Evangelism Day and through appointments you personally make, you will find that the Holy Spirit will soon begin to use you to witness and to lead people to the Lord Jesus during the course of your day. So never be without your marked, tabbed New Testament and/or your witnessing booklets.

Look for opportunities when you can be alone with someone for 30 to 60 minutes. Accept these as open doors for the Lord. After your normal contact time, start through the transition with them and continue on as the Holy Spirit leads.

Also carry your literature holder and leaflets with you at all times. Trust the Holy Spirit to open doors for you to distribute gospel literature to this person, and to that one, as you go through the day.

The author knows believers who bring someone to Christ almost every day! This can soon be the picture of your life, too!

PRESENT CHRIST TO YOUR PROSPECTS

IV. SOME PRINCIPLES TO REMEMBER

A. God's instruments for reaching a lost world

God has chosen three basic instruments with which to reach a lost world. He uses (1) the Spirit of God, (2) the Word of God, and (3) the person of God. And it takes all three! He takes a person of God, filled with the Spirit of God, effectively using the Word of God, to reach people for Christ. We can be sure of the absolute faithfulness of the first two. The third—us—has always been the unfaithful, weak link in the eternal chain for souls. Ask God to make you a *faithful* soul winner.

B. Requirements for a successful soul-winning situation

There are five requirements you must fulfill to successfully win souls.

1. *Win their confidence.* Your first big step in bringing people to Christ is to lay proper and adequate groundwork (1 Cor. 9:19-22). You must meet them, get acquainted with them, pray for them daily, and win their friendship and confidence. Only then are you ready to share with them the message of Christ. Sometimes this can be done in ten minutes and sometimes it take ten years.

2. *Use the Word of God.* Your ideas are worthless in witnessing. But God's Word is power (Heb. 4:12). So use it. You're not going to your unsaved friends to preach down to them, to argue, or to tell them what you believe. Neither are you going to them to tell them about your church, to try to change their beliefs, or to tell them about their sins. You are going to tell them about Jesus Christ as recorded in the Word of God. Use God's Word.

3. *Work with the Holy Spirit.* As you go throughout the day, as you make contact with prospects, as you begin the transition, as you present the Lord, and as you bring them to a place of decision, cooperate with the Holy Spirit. Do not try to win souls in your own strength (Lk. 24:49). You are merely an instrument of the Lord of the harvest who

You can be a Soul Winner — Here's How!

lives in you. He is the soul winner. Cooperate with Him every moment you live (Eph.5:18)!

4. *Exalt the Lord Jesus Christ.* Make your goal in life that of glorifying and exalting Him by your every word and action (Col. 3:17; 1 Cor. 10:31). Remember, you are not presenting five verses of Scripture or a plan of salvation. You are presenting the Lord of lords and the King of kings —exalt Him! Emphasize what He accomplished by His death on Calvary and emphasize ever so much His resurrection—He lives and can invade and transform lives.

5. *Draw the net.* You can find prospects, make appointments, go through the transition, present the Lord, and still never bring a person to the Lord until you draw the net. You must help them come to a place of decision. They must realize with all of their hearts that the Lord Jesus Christ stands at the door of their heart and life and they must either repent and receive Him NOW or they will automatically reject Him NOW.

V. SPECIAL SITUATIONS

A. If he says *Yes* to your question, "Do you know of any reason why you can't invite Jesus Christ into your heart?"

An answer of *Yes* at this point means (1) there's something he sincerely doesn't understand, (2) there are what he considers real problems, or (3) he's about to make an excuse. You should, first, give him a chance to explain. Hear him out. Be a good listener. Then try to help him further. Remember to use the Word of God. Also keep in mind that practically every difficulty, problem, and excuse can be answered by referring to one of the passages already used in your soul-winning plan. Be extremely wise, sincere, and humble at this point.

Additionally, you should clearly and earnestly explain to him that the only two reasons are an unwillingness to turn from sin and an unwillingness to surrender his life to Christ. Then urge him to open the door. Don't let Satan have a victory at this point. Continue on and *don't take* No *for an answer* until you are sure that he definitely is unwilling to become a Christian.

On the other hand, do not push him into something for which he is not ready or does not want. *Fruit picked before it is ripe is worthless!* It may be that you should stop, pray more earnestly, let the Spirit of God work further, and return in the future.

After he states his reason for not thinking he can invite the Lord into his heart, you might proceed with:

"I appreciate your honest response at this point, (name), but you know, regardless of the reason a person might give for not inviting the Lord in, there are only two reasons. First, an unwillingness to turn from sin, and second, an unwillingness to surrender our life to the Lord Jesus."

(Pause)

"You're willing to turn from sin, aren't you?"

"Yes."

"You're willing to surrender your life to Christ, aren't you?"

"Yes."

Now proceed on with the decision step as outlined in Chapter 3. Remember to be oh-so-tender, sincere, wise, and humble in your dealings at this very important point of conversation. You cannot be condemning or harsh. On the other hand, you must carefully let them know the truth. If he finally makes it quite plain that he does not want the Lord, conclude your time together as outlined in the following point C.

B. If he tries to put the Lord off

Once again, don't let Satan have the victory. But don't push either. Continue on until you are sure that he definitely does not want to become a Christian at this particular time. After his *No* you might proceed with:

"You plan to open the door some day, don't you, (name)?"

"Oh, sure."

"Then why not now?"

You can be a Soul Winner—Here's How!

His response at this point will be varied but continue to do all you can to urge him to make this wonderful step NOW. Pray inwardly as never before. Trust God to give victory. But do not push.

If he does finally make it quite plain that he does not want the Lord at this particular time, conclude your time together as outlined in the next point.

C. How to close if he finally says *No* to the knocking Savior

As you do soul-winning work you will have the experience of talking with people who definitely do not want the Lord at that particular time. In such cases:

1. Help them to know exactly what they are doing.
2. Leave the door open for them to later do business with the Lord personally.
3. Offer prayer.
4. Leave some appropriate literature for their consideration.
5. Leave the door open for a return visit. You might proceed something like this:

    "Remember, (name), you're not rejecting me or the church. You're saying no to the Son of God! But I do appreciate you honesty in this matter. And I am very thankful for this time together. You've been so kind and attentive.

    You know you don't need me around anyway to do business with the Lord. This matter of salvation is between you and Him. Never forget, (name), Jesus loves you, He has a wonderful plan for your life and He wants you to come to Him. Any place and at any time you can invite Him to come into your life to become your Savior and your Lord."

    (Pause)

    "Before I leave, could I offer a word of prayer?"

    "Sure."

PRESENT CHRIST TO YOUR PROSPECTS

Then you lead in prayer. Thank the Lord for the visit and for your friend's interest. Thank the Lord for His love for your friend and for all that He wants to do for him. Then pray that he will soon receive Him.

Conclude your time with him by thanking him for his time and interest. Tell him that you'll be praying for him, that you want to help him, and that you would love to talk with him again some time in the future. Leave some gospel literature with him and graciously depart.

D. How to proceed with your second visit if he says *No* to the Lord on the first visit

Do not take his *No* to the Lord on your first time together as his final word. Continue to intercede in prayer for him (Lk. 11:9-10; Isa. 59:16) (Chapter 7). Go out of your way to be with him, to win his friendship and confidence, and to show him that you love him (Chapter 8).

Make a return visit when the Holy Spirit directs. On your return visit you may consider it best to make the entire presentation again, or often you can begin with Rev. 3:20 and proceed with the decision step. In either case, make the transition by referring to your last visit and generally take up where you left off.

Some people can be won on the first visit—others take years. Do not give up whatever you do. Be faithful and leave the results to God. You are probably closer to winning him than anyone has ever been. Hold steady and stay faithful. The day *will come* when you will see him come to Christ.

E. If he says, *I don't believe the Bible*

This may be true. But in most cases he is merely repeating something that he has heard someone else say. In every case:

1. Acknowledge his statement.
2. Go ahead and use the Bible anyway.
3. Do not defend the Bible. Our job is not to defend it—our job is to proclaim it. God will vindicate and defend His

You can be a Soul Winner—Here's How!

own Word whether they believe it or not. Do not defend it—just continue to use it.

F. How to proceed if you are interrupted

If you are interrupted once or more by a telephone call, etc., as you present the Lord to the unsaved family, simply continue on from the point where you were when the interruption occurred. Remind them where you were when the interruption came and proceed from there. They may seem embarrassed because of the interruption so do all you can to graciously accept it and put them at ease.

G. How to talk with two people at one time

You should not talk with more than one person at a time unless it is a family situation such as a husband and wife. In such cases, you proceed generally the same as you would with one person except that you should alternate the verse reader. Give the Testament to the husband for the first verse, then to the wife for the second. With a family, you would then hand the Testament to the teenage son to read the third verse, etc. Get all of them personally involved in the conversation by alternating the person to whom you direct your questions, explanations, and discussion.

When drawing the net and bringing them to a decision, deal with the most hungry person first. Take him through each phase of the decision step of soul winning and see him saved. Their *yes* will encourage the others to do the same. Then turn to the other person and do the same. Take them through the assurance and initial follow-up together.

H. Gospel terminology

Do not use terms like *saved, born again,* and *Christian* unless you are talking with someone with a fundamental or evangelical background. To the average person, these terms will either have no meaning or will have a negative connotation. Simply talk to people about *knowing Jesus in a vital, personal way.*

PRESENT CHRIST TO YOUR PROSPECTS

I. If he professes to be a Christian

This may happen during the transition or at the point of decision. If your friend tells you that he is a Christian or that there was a day when he became a Christian, accept his statement but have him tell you about it.

"Oh, you are a Christian. Wonderful! Tell me about it, (name). I'd be interested to hear how you became a Christian."

At this point he will:

1. Tell you about it in a way that seems to indicate that he really did find the Lord.
2. Tell you about his confirmation or joining church, or
3. Back off, ask what you mean, and give you a chance to proceed on through the soul-winning plan as before.

If you are assured that he did meet Christ, see how all is going now in order to see further ways in which you can help him. Proceed something like this:

"Well, this is wonderful, (name). And how is your relationship and life with Christ now?"

J. If they ask about habits

During your discussion of sin (verse 1) or repentance (verse 3) or at the point of decision they may ask if giving up smoking or other habits is required or is part of becoming a Christian.

Now let's be honest with ourselves and with them. Sincere, born-again people have different convictions and standards at many points. And, too, let's remember that standards for the mature Christian are different from those of the new convert or the unsaved person considering Christ. Also, you don't know how the Holy Spirit has been speaking to them.

So don't give them a hard and fast answer. Throw it back to them with:

"What do you think, (name)?"

You can be a Soul Winner — Here's How!

If they are from a more fundamental background, they may feel that coming to Christ involves giving up smoking, drinking, card playing, etc., etc. In which case they should.

If they are from a more liberal background, they may have no idea that these things are involved. In which case for them they probably aren't. After they come to Christ and begin to walk with Him, the Spirit of God may later speak to them about some of these things. In all of these matters, the general rule is, throw it back on them and let them and the Lord work it out.

K. Backsliders

If you run into people who are backslidden, try to get them back where they belong using *their* theology and terminology.

One of Calvinist background will believe that he has lost fellowship with Christ, but not his salvation. Try to lead him back *into fellowship.* One of Arminian background will believe that he has lost his salvation. Try to lead him to *get saved again.* In both situations, point them to Jesus. Encourage them to confess and forsake their sins and to turn their lives over to Him anew.

L. How to win relatives

There is no one harder to reach than those loved ones you would like most to see come to Christ. The best thing you can do is to live a consistent, Spirit-filled Christian life and to continue to pray daily for their salvation. Be patient and steadfast; the day will come when you will be able to speak with them about their soul. You also can pray that God might use someone else to speak with them.

M. How to win members of cults

We have a tendency to categorize people: Catholics, Baptists, Jehovah Witnesses, etc., but God sees two classes of people— those with and those without Christ (1 Jn. 5:11-12). You should begin to see people the same way. Regardless of the organizational label they wear and regardless of what they believe in their head, they all have the same heart need—salvation through the Lord Jesus Christ. Use your soul-winning

PRESENT CHRIST TO YOUR PROSPECTS

plan with all classes and kinds of people—even the members of cults.

Remember, too, that you are not out to try to change their beliefs or ideas or in any way to argue or debate. Much of their erroneous theology will not change until after they are born of the Spirit. Your only job is to love them, to pray for them, and to show them what God says in His Word about their need, His wonderful provision, and how Christ can be theirs. Leave the rest to the Spirit of God.

VI. FINAL SUGGESTIONS

A. Focus on people of your own gender

If you go in pairs, two men can work with another man or with a family. A husband and wife can deal with a family, man, or woman. Two women can work with another woman. In this regard it is important to present the way of salvation to a husband and wife at the same time. Men are naturally reluctant to follow their wives. If you get the wife or children first you may lose the man. If you get the man first you'll soon have the family. So go after the husband and wife together or the man first.

B. Win people of your approximate age

Generally work with those your own age or younger.

C. Be relaxed, natural

Relax the prospect by being natural and relaxed yourself. Remember that the *Holy Spirit is the real soul winner.* Trust Him completely. He is in charge. Rest in Him.

D. Take your time

Do not be in a hurry as you use the soul-winning plan. Give the Holy Spirit time to work. Take your time as you go through the transition and *do not proceed* to the next verse *until* you know that He has made the truth of the present verse *understandable* and *personal* to your friend.

129

You can be a Soul Winner — Here's How!

E. Don't do all of the talking

Be a good listener. Let him talk. Let him tell you about his problems, etc. Talk about things of interest to him during the period of time when you're winning his (their) friendship and confidence and during the contact step of the plan.

As you use the soul-winning plan, draw your friend out. Let him read the verses. Get him personally involved as much as possible. The Holy Spirit will use this to more effectively make the truths of the verses understandable and personal to him. Ask him questions about the verses as you look at and discuss them. This is the only real way you can know whether or not the Spirit has yet made the truths of the verses understandable and personal.

F. Never argue

You have not come to argue or debate. You have come in love, to help your friend find Jesus Christ.

G. Stay on target

Don't get off the subject. Use the outlined plan to guide the conversation and to stay on target. If they ask a sincere, relevant question that appears to be important to them, you may have to stop and answer it right then. But if irrelevant questions are asked, delay answering them until after you bring the person to the Lord.

H. Always ahead to present the Lord

You are always ahead to start through the transition with your unsaved friend and to proceed through the entire soul-winning plan until:

1. The Holy Spirit signals you to stop.

2. They indicate resentment, resistance, or a desire to not discuss it further.

You and your friend are both always ahead when you present the Lord Jesus to him even if he says *No* to the Lord. You have gained additional experience in personal soul winning. You have found out more about the lost person's spiritual problems and can more effectively pray for him. You have left

PRESENT CHRIST TO YOUR PROSPECTS

gospel literature with him to read and consider. You have left the door open to see him again and to begin right where you left off.

He has probably just received the clearest presentation of the gospel thus far in his life. He knows that at least one person cares for him. He recognizes that Jesus Christ stands at the door and knocks and that he does not have Him because of his own unwillingness. And the Holy Spirit will continue to water the truth which you have presented, and the fruit will eventually come forth.

I. Finally

Through each step of the gospel presentation be compassionate and loving, gracious and courteous, wise and tactful, humble and harmless, kind and understanding, sincere and patient, and bold and courageous. *Be like Jesus!*

Questions to Answer

1. What procedure do you use with those who are not yet ready to come to Christ?
2. How do you win members of cults to the Lord Jesus?
3. How do you proceed if they say they don't believe the Bible?

Questions for Meditation and Application

1. How can you begin immediately to apply to your own life the principles you are learning from studying this book?
2. How can you rearrange your weekly schedule to allow for one evening a week for personal evangelism?
3. How can you begin to apply the principles given in section IV of this chapter to your life?

Assignment

1. Become the Holy Spirit's instrument for informal witnessing during the course of your day.
2. Set aside one evening a week for personal evangelism.

You can be a Soul Winner—Here's How!

Chapter 10

Conserve the Fruit of Evangelism

The importance of conserving the fruit of evangelism, commonly called follow-up, cannot be overemphasized! The future state of the Christian's soul and his effectiveness for Christ, the forward thrust of the church, and the condition of the world depend upon it! The Lord's work was established and advanced in the first century because of Paul's follow-up letters and visits (Acts 15:36, 18:23: 1 Th. 2: 7-16; Col. 1:28; etc.).

Our job is to make disciples (Mt. 28:19-20), not just to evangelize. Ahead lies the task of helping them acclimate to all that is a part of being a disciple.

I. PURPOSES OF FOLLOW-UP

A. Help the new convert get established.

Our first purpose in follow-up is to help the new convert to get established in his walk with Jesus.

Some short-range objectives in helping him get established include:

1. *Assurance of salvation.* Help them have assurance of their salvation. And, of course, you may have to help them several times with this. Just because they have the assurance today doesn't mean that a week from now they'll still have the assurance. This is one place where Satan tries to attack the new convert the most—to get him to lose the assurance of his salvation. He doesn't feel the same today as he did yesterday, so he must have lost his salvation. So you may have to help him several times at this point until he really once and for all has a real assurance that what he has is his.

2. *Literature.* Give them a short booklet especially written for the new Christian.

133

You can be a Soul Winner — Here's How!

3. *Daily devotions.* Get them started in daily devotions. This is something you may have to help with several times. Just because they start doesn't mean they'll continue to have daily devotions.

4. *Tell someone.* Encourage them to tell somebody what Jesus has done for them.

    These first items should be done at the very time that you lead them to the Lord. (See initial follow-up in Chapter 3.)

5. *Public profession.* Encourage them to make a public profession in one of the church services of what they've done privately in their home. You'll have to explain this to them: the purpose of it, how it's done in that particular church, etc. One way that some churches have done it is that the person who leads them to the Lord will invite them to sit together with them. Then at the end of the service, along with an invitation for other things, a very specific invitation can be given, "Those who have recently turned their lives over to the Lord, please come up so that we may introduce you to the congregation." The person who has led them to the Lord then brings them and introduces them to the congregation. And then they are given an opportunity to share a word of testimony.

6. *A new convert's class.* Get them tied in to the new convert's class. (More on that in Section II-E.)

7. *Water baptism.* Encourage them to be baptized in water.

8. *The infilling of the Holy Spirit.* Encourage them to begin to seek God for the baptism of the Holy Spirit.

9. *Tied into a church.* Our first goal is to get the gospel out to everybody, everywhere. Secondly, to get saved those who are ready. Our third goal should be to help the new Christian get established, regardless of his church background or church attendance. Fourthly, as the Lord leads, some of them will tie into a church. The Holy Spirit will lead them. Many of them will end up in your church. But it is important to have our priorities in the right order and

CONSERVE THE FRUIT OF EVANGELISM

to have our motive in the right place. Then the Lord can work.

10. *Witnessing.* Get the new convert out witnessing with you. Take him along as your silent partner. Let him give his testimony. Begin to train him. If the new converts were trained in this kind of work in the beginning, think of what would happen. The churches today that are really evangelizing, in many cases it is the new converts who are doing it. Some of us seem to have so much to *unlearn* before we can begin to learn. It's easier for some folks to start right from the beginning. But this doesn't mean that we can't change. I know of people today in their sixties and seventies who are really *on fire* and are winning souls that gave it no thought a few years ago. But God has spoken to them and begun to use them.

It will take several weeks to several months to see these ten short-range goals accomplished.

B. Teach all

A second purpose for follow-up is to teach your converts *everything* that Jesus has taught you. In Mt. 28:20 (NIV), Jesus says, "Teaching them to obey everything I have commanded you . . ." This will take a year or two of diligent discipling by a number of means (see the following Section II).

C. Mature Christian

Our third goal is to see each new Christian become a mature, Spirit-filled, producer of reproducers. In Col. 1:28 we find that Paul's goal was to "present every man perfect (complete, mature, full-grown) in Christ." Each of us have been born again in order to become like Jesus (Rom. 8:29). That should be our twofold goal—to become like Jesus ourselves—and then see our converts do the same.

II. MEANS OF FOLLOW-UP

A. At the time of conversion

Your follow-up task begins at the very same time that your friend finds the Lord and is especially important during the

You can be a Soul Winner — Here's How!

first few weeks of his Christian life. See Chapter 3 for the details of what to do at the time of his conversion.

B. A follow-up prayer list

One of Paul's methods of follow-up was prayer (Rom. 1:9; Eph. 1:16; Phil. 1:4, 9; Col. 1:3; etc.). So remember to diligently pray for those that you have the privilege of leading to the Lord.

C. Follow-up visits

One of Paul's methods of follow-up of his converts was to revisit them (Acts 15:36). So, likewise, one of your means of follow-up will be to visit those whom you lead to Jesus.

Your visits might go something like this:

1. *First follow-up visit*
    a. Have a time of general conversation.
    b. Inquire as to their progress.
        1.) Do they still have the assurance?
        2.) Are they started on daily devotions?
        3.) Have they yet told someone about what Jesus has done for them?
    c. Then introduce new items (as appropriate).
        1.) Bible study material—introduce and work on.
        2.) Explain about making public profession.
    d. Answer their questions.
    e. Have prayer together.
2. *Second follow-up visit*
    a. Have a time of general conversation.
    b. Inquire as to their progress.
        1.) Things in general.
        2.) Bible study material.
        3.) Other items from above as appropriate.
    c. Answer their questions.
    d. Have prayer together.

CONSERVE THE FRUIT OF EVANGELISM

3. *Third and subsequent visits.*

    a. Have a time of general conversation.

    b. Continue to meet with them approximately once a week until they:

        1.) Are consistently having daily devotions.

        2.) Have made a public profession of their faith.

        3.) Have completed the first study booklet.

        4.) Are part of a Bible study group for new converts.

        5.) Are part of a fellowship of believers.

    c. Answer their questions.

    d. Have prayer together.

D. Under someone's wing.

Each new convert should be placed under someone's *wing*. It may be the one who led them to the Lord. Or it may be someone else. But someone should be *personally responsible* for their development.

1. Work very closely with him until you see all of the short-range objectives under section I-A accomplished.

2. When he is consistently having his daily quiet time, is tied to a new convert's class, and is tied into a church, you can begin to cut the ties—but not completely.

    Continue to work with him until there are four generations—see Chapter 11.

All of this takes time but you can find it if you want to and if you make the best use of your time. Have a coffee break with your new Christian brother if you work at the same place, and spend the time discussing the things of Christ. Invite him for an occasional meal. Go fishing or golfing together. Telephone him.

Remember that new converts are just babes in Christ. They have much to learn. Their ideas, convictions, and standards may be completely different from yours. Do not judge, criticize, condemn, or rebuke them. Only accept, love, pray for, and help them.

137

You can be a Soul Winner — Here's How!

E. A class for new converts.

A class especially for new Christians is an absolute necessity in your friend's life. Regular Sunday school classes and worship services, aimed at the more mature Christian, will not give him the help he needs in the first few months of his Christian life. If your church does not have such a class, you take the responsibility of beginning one at least for your own converts. Remember, follow-up of those you bring to Christ is your responsibility.

The class should meet one hour a week for a period of at least six months. Here he will learn the basic principles of walking with the Lord. Together, new Christians will cover Bible study material to learn the why and how of such important topics as Bible study, prayer, resisting temptation, witnessing, stewardship, the local church, follow-up, the Spirit-filled life, family life, and the Christian's responsibility to his society and to the world. Use self-discovery, question-and-answer type, or inductive Bible study material if possible. Have the members do the study on their own at home so that a large portion of the class time can be spent in question and answer and discussion sessions. Additionally, the instructor should spend time weekly with the individual class members to help them with personal problems.

This will be a combination of classroom and practical sessions led by the pastor and leading laymen in the church. Here the members will be taught how to do inductive Bible study, how to lead others to Christ, how to bring simple gospel messages, how to effectively pray, and how to memorize Scripture. This training should then be put to immediate use through small group Bible study, Scripture memory, and prayer cells; an evening a week for evangelism; and other evangelism projects such as jail preaching, hospital visitation, tract racks for public places, tract distribution at fairs, etc.

III. CONTINUED TRAINING

In addition to the class for new Christians and your personal follow-up efforts with your friend, there should be a local-church-

CONSERVE THE FRUIT OF EVANGELISM

centered program of continuous training for God's people. This is the whole purpose of those called to full-time work—to perfect the believers for ministry—Eph. 4:11-12.

IV. BIBLE STUDY PLANS

Most Christians are not diligent students of the Bible because they lack a practical Bible study plan. Thus, these simple plans are given to enable you to study any book in the Bible as a unit. The author learned the basic ideas for these plans as a young Christian when he was discipled by the Navigators.

A. For the Beginner

1. *Read the book.* Spend a few weeks reading in a number of different translations and versions the book you choose to study. Try reading the entire book at one sitting each time you read to give you a glimpse of the book as a unit.

2. *Study the book, a chapter at a time.*

    a. Either summarize or outline the chapter. If you write a summary, it should be a simplified account of all that is in the chapter, written in your own words.

    b. Give the chapter a title. Decide on some title for the chapter. Try to make it a title which gives a clear indication of the major emphasis of the chapter. Also try to make it a title different from the title you would give any other chapter in the entire Bible. In this way, if you should study the whole Bible by this plan, you would have a separate and different title for every chapter in the Bible.

    c. Find the key verse. Now locate what you consider to be the verse that best summarizes the entire chapter.

    d. Apply the chapter to your own life. Go back through again and slowly meditate on all you have already learned and seen in the chapter. Ask the Holy Spirit to apply some particular truth of this chapter to your own life. Then write out a detailed application explaining exactly how you are going to make this

You can be a Soul Winner—Here's How!

truth real and personal in your own life. Find a promise to claim or a commandment to obey, find something that needs to be taken out of your life or something that needs to be added, find a pattern in someone else's life that you can follow, etc.

B. For the advanced student

1. *Read the book.* Spend a few weeks reading the book which you choose to study in a number of different translations and versions. Try to read the entire book at one sitting each time you read to give you a glimpse of the book as a unit.

2. *Outline the book.* After you have read the book through a number of times in each translation, make a broad outline of the book. Try to arrive at an outline of your own before consulting commentaries, Bible dictionaries, and other helps.

3. *Study the book, a chapter at a time.*

   a. Key thought and cross reference. Determine the key thought and try to find a parallel or cross reference passage somewhere else in the Bible for each verse in the chapter.

   b. Outline or summarize the chapter. Either summarize or outline your chapter. If you write a summary, it should be a simplified account of all that is in the chapter, written in your own words. If you outline the chapter, you will simply expand the book outline for the particular chapter on which you are working.

   c. Give the chapter a title. Decide on some title for the chapter. Try to make it a title which gives a clear indication of the major emphasis of the chapter. Also try to make it a title different from the title you would give any other chapter in the entire Bible. In this way, if you should study the whole Bible by this plan, you would have a separate and different title for every chapter in the Bible.

CONSERVE THE FRUIT OF EVANGELISM

    d. **Find the key verse.** Now locate what you consider to be the verse that best summarizes the entire chapter.

    e. **Find problems and questions.** Go through the chapter again, a verse at a time, and write down every problem, question, and difficulty you can find. Try to find at least one thing in each verse which you question, don't quite understand, or would like to know more about.

    f. **Apply the chapter to your own life.** Go back through once again and slowly meditate on all that you have already learned and seen in the chapter. Ask the Holy Spirit to apply some particular truth of this chapter to your own life. Then write out a detailed application explaining exactly how you are going to make this truth real and personal in your own life. Find a promise to claim or a commandment to obey, find something that needs to be taken out of your life or something that needs to be added, find a pattern in someone else's life that you can follow, etc.

Keep all of your study notes on notebook paper and file neatly in a notebook for future use in additional study of the book and for use in a Bible study group, teaching Sunday school, or speaking. (See Appendix J for other helpful Bible study materials.)

C. Bible study group suggestions

Use the following suggestions to begin a home Bible study group.

1. *Ask God to bring together a group of six to eight people who will meet for an hour or two once each week.* The group can be all men, all women, married couples, or both genders of young people.

2. *Meet together in someone's home for about two hours.* Meet in a different home each week for variety. Sit in comfortable chairs arranged in a circle or around a table.

You can be a Soul Winner—Here's How!

3. *Appoint a different leader for each meeting.* The leader will call the meeting to order and ask someone to open with prayer.

4. *Begin with some short New Testament book.* Read the entire book through in many different translations. Also read some background material on the book. Spend your first meeting discussing the book background and general contents.

5. *Then each member of the group will study the book at home during the week*, a chapter at a time, using one of the plans, or a variation of the plans, given in this chapter.

6. *The leader will lead, but not monopolize or teach*, the group in a discussion of the various sections (summary, application, etc.) of the study.

7. *Conclude with a time of prayer.*

Questions to Answer
1. What are the three purposes of follow-up?
2. What are the ten short-range objectives?
3. What are some means by which you can follow-up your converts?

Questions for Meditation and Application
1. How can you improve your follow-up efforts?
2. What can your church do to more effectively help new Christians get established in their new life? What does the Lord want you to do to get something started?
3. Is the program and approach of your church bringing believers to a place of maturity in Christ which results in personal stability, growth, and reproduction? What changes should be made in order to accomplish this task?

Assignment
1. Follow-up those you help to the Lord until they are mature, Spirit-filled, soul-winning Christians.

Part Three
Continue to Win Souls

You can be a Soul Winner—Here's How!

Chapter 11

Train Others

Your first task is to be an effective, Spirit-filled personal soul winner. This will take about a year of diligent, consistent, faithful contacting, praying, cultivating, going, and winning

Your second task is to follow-up your converts. This begins the very day you lead your first soul to Christ and continues until each one is a mature, Spirit-filled, soul-winning Christian.

Your third task is to mobilize—inspire, train, and lead—other Christians to also become soul winners. This task begins as soon as you've had the experience of bringing a few to the Lord. Begin with your own converts and expand to help others. If you're a denominational leader, begin to mobilize other denominational leaders. If you're a pastor, begin to mobilize other pastors. If you're a layman, begin to mobilize other laymen. Give them a copy of this book to study and take them with you as your silent partner. Then you go as their silent partner and observe and evaluate their efforts.

Your fourth task is to mobilize these you have trained to in turn train others. This means four spiritual generations—you, those you have trained, those they have trained, and the third generation's converts—and is based on the principle of spiritual reproduction set forth in Dt. 4:9, 6: 1-2; Isa. 58:12; 2 Tim. 2:2; and alluded to in other passages.

This principle of spiritual reproduction is one of the missing links to world evangelization. If you were the only Christian in the world today and you led one soul to Christ in the next six months, and then stayed with him until both of you did the same the next six months, the entire world would be evangelized in *approximately 16 years* as shown on the following chart.

You can be a Soul Winner—Here's How!

Six month period	Number of Christians
1	2
2	4
3	8
4	16
5	32
6	64
7	128
8	256
9	512
10	1,024
11	2,048
12	4,096
13	8,192
14	16,384
15	32,768
16	65,536
17	131,072
18	262,144
19	524,288
20	1,048,570
21	2,097,140
22	4,194,280
23	8,388,560
24	16,777,100
25	33,554,200
26	67,108,400
27	134,216,000
28	268,432,000
29	536,864,000
30	1,073,720,000
31	2,147,440,000
32	4,294,880,000
33	8,589,760,000

TRAIN OTHERS

Stick with your converts until there are four generations. In this way you can get the gospel to every person in your community. By this procedure we can fulfill the Great Commission—the message of Christ to every person in the world—in this generation.

Questions to Answer
1. What does the Scripture have to say about spiritual reproduction?
2. What tasks are yours after you become an effective soul winner?
3. When does your task of follow-up and training begin? End?

Questions for Meditation and Application
1. Assuming that you are already bringing others to the Lord, what steps should you take to begin to mobilize others in your church and community to do the same?
2. How effectively is your church evangelizing the community? What is your church doing to train soul winners? What does the Lord want you to do to help bring about these necessary changes?
3. How can the gospel be gotten to every person in the world in this generation? What part does God have for you in the accomplishment of this great task?

Assignment
1. Let God use you to bring the lost to Christ. Then begin to mobilize other Christians to do the same.
2. Believe God to give you a world-wide ministry.

147

You can be a Soul Winner — Here's How!

Chapter 12

Keep Going

There are many beginners, but not very many finishers. Anyone can start the race, but who will finish? This book may be the tool God uses to get you started in bringing others to Jesus Christ, but will you still be winning souls when you go to meet the Lord?

I. KEEP A VISION

A. Of the lost condition of men without Christ.

B. Of your responsibility for them.

C. Of how to fulfill your responsibility.

D. Of God's part.

II. KEEP SPIRIT FILLED

A. Make sure, moment-by-moment, that you are without offense toward God and toward man, that there is nothing in your life displeasing to the Lord, and that all is surrendered to Him.

B. Be faithful in your morning devotions.

C. Continue to walk through the day with the Lord.

D. Be faithful in ending your day with the Lord.

III. KEEP LEARNING

A. Continue to study this book.

B. Go with other more experienced soul winners.

C. Keep learning by being the soul-winner member of a team.

D. Put all that you learn to immediate practice.

IV. KEEP LOCATING PROSPECTS

A. Continue to locate prospects through your church.

B. Continue to locate prospects through your daily living.

C. Keep making appointments.

You can be a Soul Winner—Here's How!

V. KEEP PRAYING

A. Make private prayer a regular part of your daily life.

B. Become part of an intercessory prayer group.

C. Pray regularly for your church, your leaders, your converts, your family, and a world that is lost.

VI. KEEP CULTIVATING

A. Keep getting in touch with unsaved people.

B. Keep winning their friendship and confidence.

C. Be a friend of sinners.

VII. KEEP GOING

A. Continue to go one evening each week.

B. Keep looking for opportunities throughout the day.

C. Keep using your soul winning and visitation plans.

D. Always cooperate with the Holy Spirit.

E. Always exalt the Lord Jesus Christ.

F. Keep drawing the net.

G. Be faithful. You be faithful—leave the results with the Lord.

H. Have some goals (see Appendix B).

VIII. KEEP HELPING NEW CONVERTS AND REPRODUCING

A. Continue to work with your converts until they are mature, Spirit-filled, soul-winning Christians.

B. Continue training other Christians to be effective, Spirit-filled, personal soul winners.

KEEP GOING

Questions for Meditation and Application

1. What have you learned from this book? How are you going to begin to apply it?
2. How much of the contents of this book has become a part of your life? How can you make sure that, as the months go by, you increasingly master and make a part of your life the principles set forth herein?
3. Will you still be winning souls when you go to meet the Lord?

Assignment

1. Keep going.

You can be a Soul Winner — Here's How!

Appendix A – Definitions

Evangelism—To effectively communicate (present so that it is understood) the Good News of Christ and His salvation to a person (or group of people) so that he (they) can intelligently and willfully make a decision.

Personal Evangelism—An individual Christian communicating the gospel (Christ and His offered way of salvation) to an unsaved person.

Personal Witnessing—A Christian telling to an unsaved person a portion of that which he "has seen and heard," i.e., that of God and Christ which he has experienced personally. It is usually not as inclusive or pointed as personal evangelism.

Personal Soul Winning—The act of a Christian actually leading an unsaved person to Christ or into an experience of salvation.

Lay Evangelism—Any evangelism work done by laymen, but commonly referring to personal evangelism done by laymen.

Mass Evangelism—An individual Christian communicating the gospel to a group of unsaved people.

Total Evangelism—To effectively communicate the gospel to every person in a given area.

Appendix B – Standards for Soul Winners

As you continue to discipline your life for personal growth and outreach, it will be helpful to establish some specific standards or goals. This can most meaningfully be done in the form of a covenant with God.

The standards given here are considered to be challenging and yet quite practical and realistic for the average Christian. Consider making them yours. If they are not realistic for you, change them so they are.

By God's grace, I will faithfully do the following as long as I live:

1. Have personal devotions every morning.
2. Have a ministry of intercessory prayer.
3. Read through the Bible every year.
4. Participate in a weekly Bible study group.
5. Memorize one verse of Scripture every week.
6. Walk in the Spirit every day.
7. Pass out one gospel leaflet each day.
8. Witness each day as the Holy Spirit gives opportunity.
9. Fast and pray one day each week.
10. Spend one evening a week doing personal evangelism.
11. Follow-up all converts until they are mature, Spirit-filled, soul-winning Christians.
12. Train a new soul winner every two months.
13. Spend one-half a day with the Lord monthly.
14. Be committed to evangelizing the world in this generation, whatever the cost.

_____   _____
Date   Signed

Appendix C – Sample Prospect Card

Age of parents	House number
18 30 / 31 45 / 46 UP	Street name

	Phone	Best time to call: AM / AFT / PM / SAT / SUN

1. Last name

2. Occupation — Responsible worker

3. First name	Age	4. Church attendance		5. Sunday School attendance	
		R	O	R	O
			Where		Where
Husband					
Wife					
Children (Oldest first)					
Others					

Remarks

Census taker	Date

*You are free to reproduce this card, or you may choose to order a supply from PTWP—see page 175. We suggest that you enlarge it to a standard 5"x8" size.

RECORD OF ALL VISITS		
Date	Workers	Important Information

*You are free to reproduce this card.

Appendix D – Door-to-Door Witnessing Assignment Sheet

Team Members _____

Date_____

Area to cover:

N
↑

Start at any corner and cover all four sides of this block

Team Report:

1. Describe the portion of the block that you covered.

_____

_____

_____

_____

_____

2. Other remarks _____

_____

_____

_____

_____

*You are free to reproduce this sheet.

Appendix E – Door-to-Door Community Religious Survey

APPROACH

1. Greeting: **Hi, hello, good afternoon,** etc.
2. Tell where from: **We are from the** (name of) **church at** (location of church).
3. Explain purpose: **We are taking a Community Religious Survey.**
4. Ask cooperation: **Can you take a minute and answer a few questions for us?**
   Yes _____   No _____

SURVEY

1. Are you a member of any religious group? Yes _____ No _____

2. Would you care to give us the name of this group? _____
   _____

3. How often do you attend the meetings of this group? _____
   _____

4. According to your understanding, who is Jesus Christ? _____
   _____

5. What would you say a person must do to get to heaven? _____
   _____

6. Would you like to see what the Bible teaches about this? _____
   Now? _____ Later? _____ When? _____ (day and time)

7. Name _____Phone _____
   Address _____

(Interviewer complete between this house and the next.)

Age of parents: 18-30 _____   31-45 _____   46-up _____

Best time to call: _____

Literature left: _____

Other information: _____

Name of interviewer(s) _____ Date _____

*You are free to reproduce this sheet.

Appendix F – Telephone Community Religious Survey

APPROACH

1. Greeting: **Hi, hello, good afternoon,** etc.
2. Tell where from: **I am calling from** (name of) **church at** (location of church).
3. Explain purpose: **We are taking a Community Religious Survey.**
4. Ask cooperation: **Can you take a minute and answer a few questions for us?**

   Yes _____   No _____

SURVEY

1. Are you a member of any religious group? Yes _____ No _____

2. Would you care to give us the name of this group? _____

   _____

3. How often do you attend the meetings of this group? _____

   _____

4. According to your understanding, who is Jesus Christ? _____

   _____

5. What would you say a person must do to get to heaven? _____

   _____

6. Would you like us to come to your home and share with you what the Bible teaches about this?   Yes _____   No _____

   When would be a good time? (make an appointment)_____

   If they are not open to a visit, you may want to ask:

7. May we send you a leaflet that explains what a person must do to get to heaven?   Yes _____ No _____ (check to make sure you have the correct address)

8. Name _____ Phone _____

   Address _____

Other information: _____

Name of interviewer(s) _____ Date _____

*You are free to reproduce this sheet.

Appendix G
Reaching Cities for Christ

We believe that any city can be reached for Christ in a few years. It will take four things—

1. The Body of Christ coming together in functioning unity. This means a coming together of all involved in ministry/leadership—pastors, para-church leaders, house church leaders, authors, intercessors, etc.—such as GOD is doing in many cities around the world.

2. All believers released and mentored to their destiny—Eph. 4:11-12. All believers need to be released to be who they are in GOD—and mentored toward their destiny. This is what Eph. 4:11-12 is all about—we are to equip the saints for THEIR ministry. It's their ministry that needs to come into focus—and we need to be coaches.

3. All believers challenged and trained to reach their world. This will include training them to be personal soul winners. I believe that GOD is about to release a new wave of evangelism. I am believing GOD for millions of soul winners to be raised up around the world.

4. There needs to be a functioning representative of the Body of Christ in each neighborhood. The spiritual leaders of the city need to encourage all believers to find the other believers in their neighborhood, work place, etc. These groupings of believers in each neighborhood, work place, etc., need to be encouraged to begin meeting together once a month to get better acquainted, pray for one another, begin to pray for the neighborhood, begin to meet the needs in the neighborhood, and literally be the Body of Christ in the neighborhood. In time they will begin to see others coming to Christ through their servant-witness.

As thousands of believers become Spirit-led soul winners, and as the neighborhood and work place fellowships begin to reach out in each neighborhood and work place, the city will literally be reached for Christ.

Appendix H
Recommended Reading

A World to Win. Krupp, Nate. Bethany Fellowship Publishers, Minneapolis, MN 55438, 1966. About reaching the whole world through personal evangelism.

Born to Reproduce. Trotman, Dawson. NavPress, Colorado Springs, CO 80901. We are born-again to see others born-again.

Bring 'em Back Alive. Lehmann, Danny. YWAM, Honolulu, HI 96822. Principles of evangelism.

Catching Men. Nee, Watchman. Christian Literature Crusade, Fort Washington, PA 19034.

Cooperative Evangelism. Ferm, Robert. Zondervan Publishing, Grand Rapids, MI 49506, 1958. About Christians working in unity to reach the lost.

Evangelism Explosion. Kennedy, James. Tyndale House, Wheaton, IL, 1970. A text book on how to present the gospel.

Evangelism in the Early Church. Green, Michael. Eerdmans Publishing, Grand Rapids, MI, 1970. A thorough treatise on the subject.

Every-Member Evangelism. Conant, J.E. Harper and Brothers, New York, NY, 1922. The need to mobilize the whole church for soul winning. A classic!

Exploring Evangelism. Taylor, Mendell. Nazarene Publishing House, Kansas City, MO 64141, 1964. A large textbook on the theology, history, and methods of evangelism.

Finding Faith: A Self-Discovery Guide for Your Spiritual Quest. McLaren, Brian D. Zondervan Publishing, Grand Rapids, MI 49506, 1999. A good book to give to someone who has issues with a traditional Christian world-view yet has a desire to discover faith.

Great Personal Workers. Whitesell, Faris. Moody Press, Chicago, IL, 1956. Biographical sketches of some great soul winners.

How to Have a Soul-Winning Church. Edwards, Gene. Gospel Publishing House, Springfield, MO 65802, 1962. A call for aggressive local church-based personal evangelism.

Lifestyle Evangelism. Aldrich, Joe. Multnomah Publishers, Sisters, OR 97759, 1993.

More Ready Than You Realize: Evangelism as Dance in the Postmodern Matrix. McLaren, Brian D. Zondervan Publishing, Grand Rapids, MI 49506, 2002. A fresh look at evangelism in postmodern culture with emphasis on disciple-making as conversation, as friendship, as influence, as invitation, as companionship, as dance, as something you get to do. Challenges the notion of evangelism as sales pitch, as proof, as argument, as something you have to do.

Multiplying Disciples. Moore, Waylon. Missions Unlimited, Tampa, FL 33604, 1981. About the New Testament method of church growth.

Natural Church Development. Schwartz, Christian. ChurchSmart Resources, Carol Stream, IL, 1999. About growing healthy churches.

New Testament Follow-up. Moore, Waylon. Eerdmans Publishing, Grand Rapids, MI 49502, 1963. The practical nurture of new Christians.

Out of the Salt Shaker & into the World. Pippert, Rebecca. IVP, Downers Grove, IL 60515, 1999. Very good on friendship evangelism.

Power Evangelism. Wimber, John. Harper & Row, San Francisco, CA, 1986. The signs and wonders aspect of evangelism.

Principles of War—a Handbook of Strategic Evangelism. Wilson, Jim. PO Box 9754, Moscow, ID 83843.

Putting Your Faith on the Line. Mitchell, Hubert. Here's Life Publishers, San Bernardino, CA, 1981. How to use the telephone to evangelize.

Share the New Life with a Jew. Rosen, Moishe and Ceil. Moody Press, Chicago, IL, 1976. A study guide on evangelizing Jewish people.

Soul-Winning Laymen. Stenbock, Evelyn. Beacon Hill Press, Kansas City, MO, 1972. Stories about contemporary soul-winning laymen.

Spirit-Directed Witnessing. Cox, Martin. Wesley Press, Marion, IN, 1960. An excellent study guide on witnessing.

The Cross and Sanctification. Hegre, Ted. Bethany Fellowship Publishers, Minneapolis, MN 55438, 1960. About the Spirit-filled life, so important for the soul-winner.

The Master Plan of Evangelism. Coleman, Robert. Revell, Old Tappan, NJ 07675, 1963. Jesus' strategy for world evangelization. A classic!

The Need of the Hour. Trotman, Dawson. NavPress, Colorado Springs, CO 80901, 1957. A challenge to be the person that God can use.

The Soul-Winner's Fire. Rice, John. Sword of the Lord Publishers. Murfreesboro, TN 37130, 1941. Having a heart burning for souls.

The Soul Winners Secret. Brengle, S.L. Salvation Army Supplies, 30840 Hawthorne Blvd., Rancho Palos Verdes, CA 90275.

Unto His Own. Gartenhaus, Jacob. International Board of Jewish Missions, Atlanta, GA, 1965. A study guide on evangelizing Jewish people.

With Christ in the School of Disciple Building. Wilson, Carl. Zondervan Publishing, Grand Rapids, MI 49506, 1976. A study of Christ's method of building disciples.

You Can Witness with Confidence. Rinker, Rosalind. Zondervan Publishing, Grand Rapids, MI 49506, 1962. Practical witnessing know-how.

Appendix I
Outstanding Quotations about Soul Winning

By Arthur C. Archibald, pastor, author of the book *New Testament Evangelism,* and one of the pioneers in the field of visitation evangelism.

It is a tragic blunder to identify evangelism with any particular type or method, particularly with that type known as revivalism. Revivals and the vogue of itinerate evangelists were essentially a nineteenth century product. They grew out of camp meeting customs and the ways of the pioneer preachers. On the whole, they served their day and generation well. But that day has passed.

The man who is too busy to win souls is too busy to be a minister. The minister must know more about evangelism, and actually do more about evangelism, than any layman in his church. If he does not, how can he lead his men to achieve?

How to marshall, organize and lead forth a church into victorious saving of men—are our young ministers being taught this?

Paul goes to Ephesus and preaches two years. Yes, but he does much more. He gathered his converts into a school of training and sent them out; so that he could say, "That all they that dwell in Asia have heard the word of the Lord," something that would have been impossible had Paul preached alone.

We profess that evangelism is our chief task; but with a few exceptions our churches are organized for everything except our central project. Ninety-nine percent of our churches do not even have a standing committee or board of evangelism. We organize for worship, and what vast gains we have made in recent years! We have organized for music, and what splendid choirs we possess! We are organized for missions and our women's societies teem with vitality. We are organized for finance—how we are organized! But when it comes to the central project of the church, that for which it may be said the church primarily exists, we are almost competely minus of any organization, as bare of organization as though evangelism never even entered our thought. I wonder at times how deeply it does.

Unless we can arouse our Christian laymen to consecrate their witness in a direct effort to bring their neighbors and business associates to Christ, we will have to write off, as far as the kingdom of God is concerned, most of our modern manhood."

By Robert E. Coleman, Professor of Evangelism at Asbury Seminary, and author of *The Master Plan of Evangelism*:

Is not the spread of this vicious Communistic philosophy, in some measure, a judgment upon the church, not only upon our flabby commitment to evangelism, but also upon the superficial way we tried to go about it?

We must learn this lesson again today. There can be no dilly-dalling around with the commands of Christ.

Better to give a year or so to one or two men who learn what it means to conquer for Christ, than to spend a lifetime with a congregation just keeping the program going

By J.E. Conant, Bible teacher, evangelist, and author of numerous books including *Every-Member Evangelism*:

The Great Commission, therefore, when we sum it up, is a personal command to every Christian to go into every nook and corner of his personal world, and seek, by witnessing in the power of the Holy Spirit to the Good News of God's saving grace through the shed blood of Christ, to win every lost soul in his personal world to salvation.

The Lord has given every pastor to His church that he might train the members in soul winning, even to the point of going right out onto the field with them and doing it by their side, or helping them to do it until they learn how, using the skilled ones in turn to help train the beginners, until there is a church full of skilled and successful soul winners

There is no command in the New Testament for a sinner to go to church after the gospel, but there are multiplied commands for the Church to take the gospel to the sinner. The responsibility of every Christian is not to bring the lost to church but to take the gospel to the lost.

The first thing he (Satan) did (to hinder the work of God) was to over-emphasize the distinctions in the divinely appointed division of service as finally to get an entirely equal witnessing brotherhood divided into two companies, with the great majority in one, and the small minority in the other . . . and then he worked the witnessing out of the hands of the *laity* until it was finally regarded as the exclusive right of the *clergy*.

Satan works into the church life and activity a multitude of things that need badly enough to be done, but is not the business of the Church to do, and thus steals away both consecrated time and service from the most earnest members, who are the very ones who would be first to take the gospel to the lost if they were not entangled in these multiplied forms of *church work*.

Many have been praying for years for a great world-wide revival. When the Church gets back to literal obedience to the Great Commission the answer will come!

By Horace F. Dean, one of the specialists and author of numerous books in the field of visitation evangelism:

Several church historians agree that the Jerusalem church membership at this time increased rapidly to probably 25,000. Some qualified men in this field believe that the number was far greater, but one thing is sure: the enormous growth was achieved through a determined, Spirit-filled, house-to-house campaign of personal witnessing.

This New Testament program of soul winning and church building will work wherever there is a pastor to lay hold of the plan and persists in seeing it through.

The man of God who plans to lead his church in a continuous program of neighborhood evangelism should begin at once to prepare himself to be a specialist in this field.

The gospel-preaching churches of our land do have and proclaim, thank God, the divine message, but comparatively few of these churches are using the divine method. On the other hand, many cults are making use of the divine method.

It must be obvious to each reader that we are never going to reach the lost, the unsaved and unchurched of our generation, if we continue to follow the static sort of methods we have been using in our churches.

The average church has completely failed in schooling believers in this New Testament form of person-to-person evangelism.

By Gene Edwards, author of the book *How to Have a Soul-Winning Church* and one of the personal evangelism specialists in North America today:

> We must stop inviting the lost to church. We must start inviting them to Christ!
>
> There is not a denomination in America that has a program to reach the people who will not come to church!
>
> If you want your people to engage in New Testament soul winning, then there is no alternative: many other demanding activities must be dropped.
>
> The easiest person to win to Christ is just the average American citizen. He sits around home in the evenings; he never goes to church or Sunday school; and has not worn out his vocal chords saying *No* to enlistment efforts. He has a lonely heart and a plaguing little notion in the back of his head that he needs Jesus. When he is correctly approached about his need of Jesus Christ, he responds.
>
> You eliminate the problem of excuses by simply presenting Jesus Christ as Saviour.
>
> In the beginning, when you first seriously set out to create soul winning in your church, you must isolate personal evangelism from mass evangelism, enlistment evangelism, and everything else, and concentrate on the accomplishment and mastery of this one goal.
>
> Do you realize that if every evangelistically-minded pastor in America would set this very simple goal, and then lead his people out to witness to every home, that we could probably totally evangelize North America in one or two years?

By Claxton Monro, Episcopalian rector and author of the booklets *Witnessing Laymen Make Living Churches* and *Apostolic Ministries in the Twentieth Century*:

This age calls for the prophethood of all believers. The main task of the clergyman will be to lead his laymen to accept their several ministries and to organize the congregation into an effective, disciplined, witnessing community. His ministry to the world will be mainly through his laymen. The flock needs a shepherd, but it takes sheep to beget sheep!

We believe that the witnessing fellowship of Christian laymen is destined to become in the decades ahead the new center of vitality, power, and authority of the Church—that it will speak to this age as the Bible spoke in the Protestant awakening.

We are convinced that the gulf which now exists between the pulpit and the people can be successfully bridged only by having a witnessing fellowship among the laymen. Only the revelation of Jesus Christ through the lives and hearts of believers can speak with understanding and authority to the pragmatic and cynical mentality of our age.

By Waylon Moore, Southern Baptist pastor and author of *New Testament Follow-up*:

In this day of mass dynamics and group thinking throughout our social structure, it must be constantly emphasized that our neglected spiritual resource for world evangelism is the layman who has been given adequate scriptural follow-up care. He is the shortest and most effective avenue to evangelizing the area of a church's influence.

God always intended that His work should be carried on by the individual Christian, and not left entirely to the pastor. Most of the commands in the New Testament were given to all Christians, not just to the church leaders. The longer we cling to a sharp laity-clergy division, neglecting to develop lay leadership through personal training and follow-up, the farther we lag behind in the great task of evangelizing the world.

That peer of pulpit giants, Charles Haddon Spurgeon, prayed, "Lord, give me twelve men who love souls and I'll take London from end to end!" He didn't have the twelve at that time, but God heard his prayer, and before long young men were being trained to win souls. In a few years, London was shaken with the gospel message as never before by this man and his helpers.

By Roscoe Pershall, pastor, personal evangelism specialist, and author of *You Can Win Them*:

Many of us are failing to find one of the greatest areas of effectiveness—personal evangelism.

The church loses its contact with the unsaved lives unless there is a living calling program. The longer a person is a Christian, the more he tends to find all his life in the church.

The simpler presentation (of the gospel) the more powerful it is.

Trust when in the battle. Literally trust moment by moment that He will lead you and give you strength . . . If ever a man can draw on the promises, grace and presence of the Lord it is while he is fulfilling the command to go and evangelize.

Within the modern-day Church there is a vast reservoir of potential might that is mainly untapped.

It must be on his (pastor's) heart if it is to be the heart of his church. He must win souls himself by this method. The people must see the pastor's example; they must hear of his victories and see those whom he has won, hear their testimonies.

By Paul S. Rees, world-wide Christian leader and author of many books including *Stir Up the Gift*:

The chief function of the pastor is the inspiring and training of the lay members to go out and spread the evangel. No passage in the New Testament states it better than Ephesians 4:11-12, although the full force of the apostle's thought is obscured in the Authorized Version

Our need is an inspired leadership to show us that evangelism is the primal task of the whole congregation.

Is the witnessing church re-emerging? There are signs of it. As they multiply we shall find ourselves living again in the atmosphere of the Book of Acts.

The local congregation, rooted as it is in the life of the community, must be mobilized for effective witness.

By Rosalind Rinker, author of numerous books including *You Can Witness with Confidence*:

You can win others to Christ, with confidence and with quietness. There may be some things you have to unlearn, and some things you have to learn. But with God's help you can do both.

Nothing less than the goal of being totally committed to Jesus Christ (body, soul and spirit; past, present and future) will give God the wide open door He needs to live in you and to love through you.

When we emphasize personal salvation more than a personal Saviour, we are asking people to put their trust in an experience rather than in Jesus Christ.

Argument has never won a soul! Sharing and listening, questioning and listening—with heavy emphasis on listening—will help you reach your friend and lead him on to where God wants him to be

By Dawson Trotman, founder of the Navigators and author of the booklets, "Born to Reproduce" and "The Need of the Hour":

Soul winners are not soul winners because of what they know, but because of Whom they know and how well they know Him and how much they long for others to know Him.

The gospel spread to the known world during the first century without radio, television or the printing press, all because these produced ones were producing. But today we have a lot of pew-sitters—people who think that if they are faithful in church attendance, put good-sized gifts into the offering plate, and get people to come, they have done their best.

Let me tell you what I believe the need of the hour is. Maybe I should call it the answer to the need of the hour. I believe it is an army of soldiers, dedicated to Jesus Christ, who believe not only that He is the Son of God, but that He can fulfill every promise He has ever made, and that there isn't anything too hard for Him. It is the only way we can accomplish the thing that is on His heart —getting the gospel to every creature.

"All power in heaven and earth is Mine. It's Mine for you to appropriate." This is not only a privilege; it's an order. He wants nothing less. God doesn't want you to take an island . . . He wants you to take a world. For what are you asking God? What do you want? Do you want to win a few? You'll have to start with a few, and you'll have to be successful with a few. You can because Jesus said, "Follow Me, and I will make you fishers of men." No man ever followed Jesus who didn't become a fisher of men. He never fails to do what He promised. If you're not fishing, you're not following. You have to win one before you win five, and five before you can win five hundred. The world is before you. How big is your faith?

The need of the hour is men who want what Jesus Christ wants and believe He wants to give them the power to do what He has asked. Nothing in the world can stop those men. Do you believe that? Do you want to be one of them?

By others:

"Men are God's method. The Church is looking for better methods; God is looking for better men." *E.M. Bounds*

"I care not how or where I live or what hardship I go through— so that I can but gain souls." *David Brainerd*

"We have developed a spectator Christianity in which a few speak and many listen. The New Testament Church commenced with Jesus saying to everyone of His followers, apostles and ordinary believers alike, 'Go ye into all the world and preach the gospel.' These words were not spoken in a pastor's conference or in a seminary classroom. They were spoken to all His disciples. But what started as a lay movement has deteriorated into a professonal pulpitism financed by lay spectators." *Howard Butt*

"The failure to witness has also given rise to other problems besides lack of soul winning. The Church, neglecting to emphasize outreach for souls, has often turned to other lesser emphases. In a desperate attempt to gain acceptance and become 'known,' peripheral ideas are stressed. This has only served to increase tensions both with the outside and on the inside. Consequently we often become known for the things we do not believe in rather than for the positive truths of God's Word.

"To all of this idea that witnessing is for a limited group and that it is a highly specialized operation, we must take sharp exception. We are convinced that God expects personal soul winning in every Christian's life." *Martin W. Cox*

"The greatest need of the human soul is to be loved." *Robert Ferm*

"It was emphasized that the commands of the Word of God demand: . . . The total mobilization of every member of the church. It is not a question of the few being especially chosen and sent forth, but rather that every born-again person is obligated to join the army of God for world conquest. This means mobilizing all our resources of manpower, means and money for one express purpose—to take the gospel to every living soul in this generation." *Report from IFMA Congress on World Mission held in December 1960*

"I must speak to one soul each day about Christ." *D.L. Moody*

"A layman said to me recently, 'your job is like that of a foreman in a plant. A foreman has a twofold responsibility. First, he must teach and train his men to do their work. Second, he must watch over them, guiding and encouraging them to produce. So, you as a clergyman have to train us for our ministry, and then help us to fulfill our mission, to produce. We are called to go and bear fruit; you are called to see that we do it.' Without introducing yet another term to describe the role of the clergyman, we can see that he is indeed a foreman to his people. He must train his people for their ministry and work with them as they discover their mission. Typically, he must work in depth with a few persons at a time until the few become lay-foremen able to train others and thus share the ministry.

"If the clergyman is truly to be the foreman to his people, his commitments and responsibilities must be tailored to this function. He must be willing to do less than he ought in other aspects of his ministry in order that he may do more of what he ought to fulfill his chief task. The recovery of mission for the clergyman may mean significant revision of the priorities in his daily schedule." *Robert A. Raines*

"The simplest way to embarrass a normal congregation is to ask them two ordinary questions: (1) When did you last lead someone else to Christ? (2) When did you last try?

"All Christians are called to be evangelists." *W.E. Sangster*

"It is amazing how many Christians have never given a clear and positive witness for Christ to say nothing of having won a soul to Him." *Lorne Sanny*

"If a seeker can get you into an argument, you are done.

"Unless the Holy Spirit is cooperating with you nothing will happen." *Oswald J. Smith*

"One of the great tragedies of the church has been its failure to cultivate the seeking attitude.

"The church should be the pastor's force, not his field of labor." *J. Edgar Smith*

"Our ministry today is restricted by our unscriptural methods. We leave the primary responsibility of evangelism to a few paid pastors, Bible teachers, evangelists and missionaries. Our strongest method is in inviting an evangelistic party at great financial expense to conduct huge evangelistic campaigns. We sink millions of dollars in costly church buildings and invite the people to come in and hear the gospel. Not so in the early church.

"Every believer should realize that no matter what his employment is it is only paying his expenses to be an ambassador for the Lord Jesus Christ." *James A. Stewart*

"When the church loses compassion, Christianity confines itself to acts of worship; but when it is filled with love for a needy world it grows from worship to activity. This is the hour for action. We can have apostolic success, if we follow the plan laid down by Christ. This is one task from which no Christian should consider himself exempt . . . Soul winning is every man's job." *George Sweeting*

"It is a great privilege to preach the gospel, but this world can be reached and evangelized far more quickly and thoroughly by personal work than by public preaching. Indeed, it can be reached and evangelized only by personal work. When the whole church of Jesus Christ shall rouse to its responsibility and privilege in this matter, and every individual Christian become a personal worker, the evangelization of the world will be close at hand. When the membership of any local church shall rouse to its responsibility and privilege in this matter, and each member becomes a personal worker in the power of the Holy Spirit, a great revival will be close at hand for the community in which that church is located." *R.A. Torrey*

"To be a good listener is one of the surest ways of winning and holding men.

"It is the hardest work in the world to do, and it always will be the hardest . . . Many a man who is eloquent before a great congregation is dumb before a single individual. . .it requires more faith and courage to say two words face to face with one single sinner, than from the pulpit to rebuke two or three thousand persons." *Charles G. Trumbull*

"Personal evangelism was the method most widely used by the early Christians as recorded in the book of Acts.

"Personal evangelism is at its best when operating in and through the New Testament local church." *F.D. Whitesell*

"He was out of breath pursuing souls." *A Wesley biographer*

"Major on mission, message, men, methods, and materials." *Bill Bright*

"We need to break out of our ecclesiastical ghettos and permeate non-Christian society. In the church's mission of sacrificial service, evangelism is primary. World evangelism requires the whole church to take the whole gospel to the whole world.

"We affirm that the church's visible unity in truth is God's purpose. Evangelism also summons us to unity, because our oneness strengthens our witness, just as our disunity undermines our gospel of reconciliation." *From the Lausanne Covenant, International Congress on World Evangelism, Lausanne, Switzerland, 1974*

"A true messenger lives a burdened life. If he is the Lord's vessel, he carries in his heart a burden for souls none can share but those who know it firsthand." *Billy Graham*

Appendix J
Other Helpful Materials from PTWP

I. PERSONAL EVANGELISM MATERIALS

Bible Studies for Soul Winners. Study this book first to get a thorough, biblical understanding of evangelism. Learn what the Bible says about –

- Sin and its consequences
- God's remedy for sin
- How man must respond to God's remedy
- Our task of evangelism
- God's part in evangelism
- Our part in evangelism
- Jesus' evangelism
- The first century church's evangelism

ISBN 1-929451-17-2 • 52 pages $8.95

You can be a Soul Winner—Here's How.!
ISBN 1-929451-13-X • 180 pages $12.95

Special Offer — *You can be a Soul Winner* and *Bible Studies for Soul Winners,* both for $19.95.

The Way to God. A 16-page witnessing booklet you can use to lead your unsaved friends to Jesus. It has been used around the world, on every continent. People have been saved just by reading it. Includes the biblical emphases of repentance and the Lordship of Jesus Christ.
ISBN 1-929451-18-0 ....$.25 ea., 10 for $2, 100 for $15

The New Birth—What It Is, and What It Is Not. A 6-page leaflet giving a clear, in-depth presentation of the way of salvation. $.10 ea., 100 for $6.

Prospect Card. Shown in Appendix C. Use this card to keep a record of progress with your unsaved prospects. $.03 ea., 50 for $10, 100 for $18.

175

II. FOLLOW-UP MATERIALS

Basic Bible Studies. A question-and-answer type, foundational Bible study book about the Christian faith. Chapters include:

1. Is There a God?
2. The Issue of Sin
3. What Provision Did God Make for Man's Sin?
4. How Should Man Respond to God's Provision?
5. Abiding in Christ
6. The Christian and God's Word
7. The Christian and Prayer
8. The Christian and the Holy Spirit
9. The Christian and Warfare
10. The Christian and Witnessing
11. The Christian and the Home
12. The Christian and the Church
13. The Christian and Business Affairs
14. The Christian and Discipleship
15. The Christian and Service
16. The Christian and the Return of Christ

ISBN 1-929451-02-4 • 80 pages $11.95

Foundations for the Christian Life by John G. Gill. Written to give the foundation stones for the Christian life, as listed in Hebrews 6:1-3. Many Christians struggle in their Christian life because the proper foundation was not laid in the beginning. This book biblically gives this proper foundation. Questions at the end of each chapter make it even more practical.
ISBN 1-929451-11-3 • 118 pages $11.95

God's Word Puts the Wind in My Sails by Joanne Bachran. A guide to knowing GOD and His Word. It is full of helpful, basic material for all believers, especially new Christians. A reference guide, Bible study, personal devotional, and journal—all rolled into one. A personal compass for a more intimate relationship with God. Very useful!
ISBN 1-929451-08-3 • 216 pages $13.95

III. MATERIALS TO HELP YOU GROW

New Testament Survey Course. A very unique 47-lesson Bible study survey of the New Testament.

- It covers every verse of the New Testament.
- It leads you in an in-depth study of each book. You will read the entire New Testament and either answer summarizing questions or summarize the book, a paragraph at a time.
- It harmonizes the Gospels so that you study Jesus' life in a single, chronological narrative.
- It places the letters in the order in which they were actually written.
- This study gives you background information on each book of the New Testament.
- You will apply each book to your own life situation.
- You will decide on verses to memorize from each book.
- You will know the New Testament when you have finished this study!

ISBN 1-929451-03-2 • 234 pages $16.95

Mastering the Word of God—and Letting It Master You! This book is about various methods of in-depth Bible intake: how to hear, read, study, memorize, and meditate on the Word of God. With this book you will learn how to study the Bible. You will be able to develop a life-long plan of in-depth Bible study—mastering God's Word, and letting It master you.

ISBN 1-929451-04-0 • 46 pages $6.95
Workbook • ISBN 1-929451-09-1 • 34 pages $5.95

Bible Outlines. A supplemental book to *Mastering the Word of God*. This book gives an outline for every book of the Bible, a title for every chapter, and other helpful information.

ISBN 1-929451-10-5 • 62 pages $9.95

Getting to Know GOD. A devotional Bible study book on 57 aspects of GOD's Person, Character, and Attributes: His love, His mercy, His faithfulness, His goodness, His glory and majesty, etc. For each attribute, you will read an introduction, prayerfully read three or four pages of appropriate Scripture verses, answer study questions, do research, meditate on and apply the lesson to your life, memorize verses of your choice, and pray a closing prayer. This book was written by an actual Bible study group. This study will change your life!
ISBN 1-929451-05-9 • 288 pages $19.95

Qualities God is Looking for in Us. A 53-week Bible study, devotional book on the qualities God is looking for in us: abiding in Christ, boldness, contentment, diligence, discipline, early riser, forgiving, generous, holy, honest, humble, obedient, praiser, prayer, servant, wise, zealous, etc. For each quality, you will read an introduction, prayerfully read three or four pages of appropriate Scripture verses, answer study questions, do research, meditate on and apply the lesson to your life, memorize verses of your choice, and pray a closing prayer. This book was written by an actual Bible study group. This study will greatly challenge you!
ISBN 1-929451-06-7 • 384 pages $24.95

ORDER FORM

Preparing the Way Publishers

2121 Barnes Avenue SE, Salem, OR 97306, USA
Voice 503-585-4054 • Fax 503-375-8401
E-mail: kruppnj@open.org • Website: www.PTWpublish.com

PERSONAL EVANGELISM MATERIALS

QTY	TITLE	PRICE	TOTAL
_____	Bible Studies for Soul Winners $8.95	_____	
_____	You can be a Soul Winner—Here's How! $12.95	_____	
_____	Special Offer: Bible Studies/You can be a Soul-Winner ..$19.95	_____	
_____	The Way to God ....25¢ ea., 10 for $2, 100 for $15.00	_____	
_____	The New Birth ....10¢ ea., 100 for $6.00	_____	
_____	Prospect Card ....3¢ ea., 50 for $10, 100 for $18.00	_____	

FOLLOW-UP MATERIALS

_____	Basic Bible Studies $11.95	_____	
_____	Foundations for the Christian Life $11.95	_____	
_____	God's Word Puts the Wind in My Sail $13.95	_____	

MATERIALS TO HELP YOU GROW

_____	New Testament Survey Course $16.95	_____	
_____	Mastering the Word of God $6.95	_____	
_____	Workbook $5.95	_____	
_____	Bible Outlines $9.95	_____	
_____	Getting to Know GOD $19.95	_____	
_____	Qualities God is Looking for in Us $24.95	_____	

Ordering Information: Fill in your order and send it **with payment** to Preparing the Way Publishers for processing. A new copy of this Order Form will be included with your order for your future ordering use.

Payments: To avoid extra bookkeeping and handling expenses, credits for less than $1.00 will not be sent. Prices are subject to change without notice. **Full payment is expected with order.**

Postage and Handling for mainland United States orders:

Amount of Order	P & H	Postage and Handling for Alaska, Hawaii,
Under $20.00	$4.00	**U.S. possessions, and all other nations:**
$20.00 - $39.99	15%	Actual postage charge plus 10% handling
$40.00 and above	10%	

TOTAL Book Order $_____

Plus Postage & Handling $_____

GRAND TOTAL $_____

Ship To:

Name: _____ Date of Order: _____

Address: _____ Telephone: _____

City _____ State _____ Zip_____ Nation _____

Clip and mail

Preparing the Way Publishers

makes available practical materials
(books, booklets, and audio tapes)
that call the Church to the radical Christianity
described in the Bible.

Some titles include —
The Way to God
Basic Bible Studies
New Testament Survey Course
Mastering the Word of God—and Letting It Master You
Bible Outlines
Getting to Know GOD
Qualities God is Looking for in Us
Bible Studies for Soul Winners
You can be a Soul Winner—Here's How!
The Church Triumphant at the End of the Age
New Wine Skins—the Church in Transition
God's Simple Plan for His Church—a Manual for House Churches
Leadership–Servanthood in the Church as found in the New Testament
Woman—God's Plan not Man's Tradition
Restoring the Vision of the End-times Church
God's Word Puts the Wind in My Sail
Foundations for the Christian Life

For further information, see the PTW web page
at www.PTWPublish.com

Or contact —

Preparing the Way Publishers
2121 Barnes Avenue SE
Salem, OR 97306-1096, USA

phone 503/585-4054
fax 503/375-8401
e-mail <kruppnj@open.org>

CPSIA information can be obtained at www.ICGtesting.com
Printed in the USA
BVOW02s0048090913

330541BV00001B/26/A